ADVENTURES

THE CHRONICLES OF LUCIFER JONES

Volume I—1922-1926: Adventures

Volume II—1926-1931: Exploits

Volume III—1931-1934: Encounters

Volume IV—1934-1938: Hazards
(published by Subterranean Press)

Volume V—1938-1942: Voyages
(forthcoming from Subterranean Press)

THE CHRONICLES OF LUCIFER JONES

VOLUME I 1922-1926
ADVENTURES

MIKE RESNICK

an imprint of

ARC MANOR
Rockville, Maryland

The Chronicle of Lucifer Jones: Volume I—1922-1926: Adventures Copyright © 1985 by **Mike Resnick.** All rights reserved. This book may not be copied or reproduced, in whole or in part, by any means, electronic, mechanical or otherwise without written permission from the publisher except by a reviewer who may quote brief passages in a review.

This is a work of fiction. Any resemblance to any actual persons, events or localities is purely coincidental and beyond the intent of the author and publisher.

Tarikian, TARK Classic Fiction, Arc Manor, Arc Manor Classic Reprints, Phoenix Pick, Phoenix Rider, Manor Thrift and logos associated with those imprints are trademarks or registered trademarks of Arc Manor Publishers, Rockville, Maryland. All other trademarks and trademarked names are properties of their respective owners.

This book is presented as is, without any warranties (implied or otherwise) as to the accuracy of the production, text or translation.

ISBN: 978-1-61242-034-9

www.PhoenixPick.com
**Great Science Fiction & Fantasy
Free Ebook Every Month**

**Visit the Author's Website
http://MikeResnick.com**

Published by Phoenix Pick
an imprint of Arc Manor
P. O. Box 10339
Rockville, MD 20849-0339
www.ArcManor.com

This book, about my favorite fictional character,
is for Carol,
my favorite non-fictional one.

♈

CONTENTS

ME AND LUCIFER *(Introduction)*	9
CAST OF CHARACTERS	13
1. THE WHITE GODDESS	15
2. PARTNERS	29
3. THE VAMPIRE	47
4. SLAVE TRADING	61
5. THE MUMMY	76
6. A RED-LETTER SCHEME	95
7. MUTINY	106
8. AN AFFAIR OF THE HEART	120
9. THE LOST RACE	134
10. THE LORD OF THE JUNGLE	149
11. THE BEST LITTLE TABERNACLE IN NAIROBI	162
12. THE ELEPHANTS' GRAVEYARD	177

ME AND LUCIFER

Lucifer Jones was born one evening back in the late 1970s. I was trading videotapes with a number of other people—stores hadn't started renting them yet, and this was the only way to increase your collection at anything above a snail's pace—and one of my correspondents asked for a copy of H. Rider Haggard's African adventure classic She, with Ursula Andress, which happened to be playing on Cincinnati television.

I looked in my Maltin Guide and found that She ran 117 minutes. Now, this was back in the dear dead days when everyone knew that Beta was a better format than VHS, and it just so happened that the longest Beta tape in existence at the time was two hours. So I realized that I couldn't just put the tape on and record the movie, commercials and all, because the tape wasn't long enough. Therefore, like a good correspondent/trader, I sat down, controls in hand, to dub the movie (which I had never seen before) and edit out the commercials as they showed up.

About fifteen minutes into the film Carol entered the video room, absolutely certain from my peals of wild laughter that I was watching a Marx Brothers festival that I had neglected to tell her about. Wrong. I was simply watching one of the more inept films ever made.

And after it was over, I got to thinking: if they could be that funny by accident, what if somebody took those same tried-and-true pulp themes and tried to be funny on purpose?

So I went to my typewriter—this was back in the pre-computer days—and wrote down the most oft-abused African stories that one was likely to find in old pulp magazines and B movies: the elephants' graveyard, Tarzan, lost races, mummies, white goddesses, slave-trading, what-have-you. When I got up to twelve, I figured I had enough for a book . . . but I needed a unifying factor.

Enter Lucifer Jones.

Africa today isn't so much a dark and mysterious continent as it is an impoverished and hungry one, so I decided to set the book back in the 1920s, when things were wilder and most of the romantic legends of the pulps and B movies hadn't been thoroughly disproved.

Who was the most likely kind of character to roam to all points of Africa's compass? A missionary.

What was funny about a missionary? Nothing. So Lucifer became a con man who presented himself as a missionary. (As he is fond of explaining it, his religion is "a little something me and God whipped up betwixt ourselves of a Sunday afternoon.")

Now, the stories themselves were easy enough to plot: just take a traditional pulp tale and stand it on its ear. But anyone could do that: I decided to add a little texture by having Lucifer narrate the book in the first person, and to make his language a cross between the almost-poetry of Trader Horn and the totally fractured English of Pogo Possum, and in truth I think there is more humor embedded in the language than in the plots. (And as the series extended to more books, his language became a little more fractured too.)

Lucifer, bless him, isn't the brightest bulb in the lamp. Upon seeing Lord Carnavon's caravan bringing the contents of King Tut's 3,000-year-old-tomb to Cairo, only he could ask, "Just settling the estate now, are they?"

Because this was a labor of love, I also started putting in a bunch of references that would be clear only to a tiny segment of the audience. For example, in Adventures Tarzan is Lord Bloomstoke, the name Edgar Rice Burroughs originally chose for him before changing it to Lord Greystoke. Every character in Casablanca is named after a car, in honor of Claude Rains (Lt. Renault) and Sydney Greenstreet (Signore Ferrari) from the movie Casablanca. A number of the details were historically accurate: Bousbir really was the biggest whorehouse in the world in 1925, there really was a nude painting of Nellie Willoughby hanging over the Long Bar in the New Stanley Hotel in the 1920s, the Mangbetu really were cannibals, and so on.

Then, since I had leaned rather heavily on the pulps for my plotlines, I started borrowing characters from the B movies: The Rodent is a thinly-disguised Peter Lorre, Major Dobbins is Sydney

Greenstreet, the Dutchman is Walter Slezak, and so on; every one of my favorite 1940s scoundrels made it from the screen to the page.

Finally, I needed a con man who was even better at his job than Lucifer, lest the book end too soon, and so I came up with Erich von Horst, who makes very few appearances—everyone else in a Lucifer Jones book keeps showing up time and again in the oddest places—but lays a number of economic time bombs across the continent that Lucifer keeps encountering at the least opportune moments. In fact, halfway through the fifth book (where I am as I write this), von Horst has made more appearances than any other character.

The most fun I ever had in my life was the two months that I sat at the typewriter working on Adventures. I've done books of more lasting import, and I've created characters of far more depth and complexity, but during that period I fell, hopelessly and eternally, in love with Lucifer Jones.

I sat on it until I was well-established at Signet, which was publishing all my science fiction novels at the time. They didn't quite know what to do with it, so they sat on it for a couple of years and finally released it in 1985, labeling it Science Fiction, which it most decidedly is not, and implying on the cover that the Honorable Right Reverend Doctor Lucifer Jones was just another adventurous version of Doctor Indiana Jones, which he most certainly is not.

The book came out, did all right but never really found its audience, and vanished a year or two later. A few mainstream newspapers found it—one New York reviewer called it the greatest parody of the adventure novel ever written—but for the most part it didn't make any waves.

I had plotted out five more Lucifer Jones books, one on each continent (each, like Adventures, would end with the various national governments acting in concert to kick him off that particular land mass). Exploits takes place in Asia from 1926 to 1931, and includes an Insidious Oriental Dentist, a Chinese detective with too many sons, a hidden kingdom where no one grows old, an abominable snowman, a seductive criminal known as The Scorpion Lady, and the like. Encounters takes place in Europe from 1931 to 1934, and boasts vampires, werewolves, the theft of the Crown Jewels, the discovery of Atlantis, the Clubfoot of Notre Dame, and similar. Hazards takes place in South America from 1934 to 1938, amid all its lost cities, tropical jungles, and strange religious rites. Voyages has Lucifer island-hop from South America to Australia, finding lost treasures, a giant ape, naked goddesses along the way, and he also gets to explain why it's not really his fault that the Japanese bombed Pearl Harbor. And finally there will be Intrigues, set in Australia and Antarctica, at the end of which he will have been barred from every land mass in the world.

I had it all planned out when I finished Adventures—except that Signet decided they didn't want anything but true-blue science fiction, and at the time I had no other publishers. Over the next few years I moved over to Tor and Ace, and while I still longed to get back to Lucifer Jones, I was turning out serious, prestigious, award-winning stuff at all lengths, and it never occurred to me to ask if anyone was interested in him. In point of fact, I thought I was the only person who even remembered Lucifer Jones.

Until 1991, when Brian Thomsen of Warners asked me to write a book for him. I explained that I would love to—Brian and I had been friends for years, and I'd always wanted to work with him—but I was under contract to both Tor and Ace, and between them they held options for all my science fiction.

"But I'm free to sell Lucifer Jones," I added, half expecting him to ask who the hell Lucifer Jones was.

"I loved Adventures!" exclaimed Brian, and we were in business.

Warners decreed that for the price they were paying me – I was considerably more valuable then when I'd written Adventures they needed considerably more than a dozen of Lucifer's adventures. So I wrote Exploits and Encounters, handed them in, and called it The Chronicles of Lucifer Jones.

And that was it for eleven years. Then Bill Schafer of Subterranean Press asked for me to resurrect Lucifer, and he's been running him in almost every issue of Subterranean Magazine. When I'd finished a dozen South American episodes, he collected them as Hazards, and as I write these words I've done seven of the episodes for Voyages.

I've received more acclaim for other things I've written. I've won five Hugos, and I have more than one hundred trophies, scrolls, certificates and the like in my trophy room. And if someone told me I could keep them or keep writing Lucifer Jones stories but not both, I'd kiss them all good-bye without a second thought.

Lucifer remains my favorite of all my characters. I love him, and I hope after reading this book you will too.

Mike Resnick
June, 2011

CAST OF CHARACTERS

The Dutchman, who prefers to think of his slave-trading operation as an International Employment Placement Service.

Erich Von Horst, a con man's con man.

Herbie Miller, ivory poacher and part-time vampire.

Long Schmidt and *Short Schmidt*, a pair of brothers from Pittsburgh who became gods at the lost kingdom of the Malaloki.

Burley Rourke, a doctor specializing in diseases of the gullible.

Rosepetal Schultz, who differs from most ancient Egyptian queens in that she was born twenty-three years ago in Brooklyn.

The Rodent, undersized killer of either sixteen or thirty-five men, who changed his name from the Weasel for professional reasons.

Mr. Christian, officer aboard the good ship Dying Quail.

Bloomstoke, a tall, bronzed British nobleman who is living with a tribe of apes while hiding from his creditors.

Neeyora, just your typical naked blonde white goddess, who tips the scales at four hundred pounds, give or take an ounce.

Capturing Clyde Calhoun, who brings 'em back alive. Not intact, but alive.

Amen-hetep III, whose mummy carries a half-clad girl through the streets of Cairo before checking in at Shepheard's Hotel.

Major Theodore Dobbins, a man with a taste for rich widows, who is also a speculator in certain perishable commodities imported from far exotic China and points east.

And our narrator, *The Right Reverend Honorable Doctor Lucifer Jones*: his religion is a little something he and the Lord worked out between themselves one afternoon, his tabernacle is the most prosperous brothel in British East Africa, and he has serious disagreements with the authorities of fourteen different African nations over the finer points of the law. On the other hand, he means well.

1. THE WHITE GODDESS

I knew a real live vampire. It was in Africa about seventy years ago, and his name was Herbie Miller. He didn't look much like a vampire, I suppose—walked around in khaki pants that he cut off above the knees, and his hair wasn't slicked down or nothing. I can't say he was real fond of crosses, but daylight didn't bother him none, and he had no problems walking over running water, except that he couldn't swim and narrow bridges scared the hell out of him.

I don't know why he should have been so interested in me, especially considering that I was a man of the cloth back then, but he was. When he wasn't trying to nab me in the neck, which was pretty difficult inasmuch as poor Herbie was barely five feet tall with his boots on, he kept coming up with crazy schemes about how I should go to the local hospital—not Schweitzer's, but one you've probably never heard of—and borrow some blood, for which he promised to pay me in pounds or dollars or rupees or whatever else he'd gotten off one of his more recent meals.

You know, I think about Herbie and some of the others I met, and I'd have to say that even without the animals—and I never did see all that many of them anyway, except for the time I was an ivory poacher—Africa was a pretty interesting place to be back then. I had my flock and my tabernacle, and of course there was Herbie, who came smack-dab between my little business excursions into opium and brothels, and there were Long Schmidt and Short Schmidt, a pair of brothers who became gods, and there was Capturin' Clyde Calhoun and a batch of others.

Africa was full of colorful folk like that in the old days. They called themselves adventurers and explorers and hunters and missionaries, but what they mostly were were outcasts. They gathered in the civilized cities, most of them: Johannesburg, Nairobi, Mombasa, Pretoria, places like that. Every now and then they'd go out into the bush—only bad pulp writers ever called it the jungle—after everything from ivory to lost gold mines to half-naked white priestesses. A lot of them found ivory, and a few found gold, but the only man I ever knew who went into the bush and found himself a white woman was an Irishman named Burley Rourke.

I met him just a few days after I got off the boat, young and hopeful and sporting my first beard. Due to a series of unfortunate misunderstandings during an informal game of chance, I had been invited to inspect the premises of the Johannesburg gaol, which, while tastefully appointed, was nevertheless not the temporary residence I would have picked had the choice been mine.

Rourke was lying on a cot in the adjacent cell. He was a tall, cadaverous man, with bushy black eyebrows and an enormous dimple on his chin. He had the longest, whitest, most delicate fingers I had ever seen on a man, and since even his fingernails were clean, I asked him if he, like myself, was being incarcerated due to a certain flexibility toward the hard and fast rules of the game. He allowed that this was indeed the case, and I asked him if his trade was cards or dice.

"Neither," he said. "I'm a doctor, specializing in diseases of the gullible."

That's when I knew we were going to hit it off just fine.

"How about yourself?" said Rourke. "You look like some kind of preacher man, all done up in black like you are."

"Indeed I am, Brother Rourke," I said with some modesty. "I don't know how a respectable man like me got involved with all them sinful characters in the first place. I suppose I was just following the good Lord's mandate to consider every man my brother. 'Course, I never have gotten around to viewing all the women exactly as sisters."

"And what religion do you preach?" asked Rourke.

"One me and the Lord worked out betwixt ourselves one afternoon," I said.

Actually, the way I see it, my calling was determined the day I was born. We had a little farm outside Moline, Illinois, and once I was alive and secure, my mother sent my father to the county courthouse to register my name, which was to be Lucas Jones or Lucius Jones, I'm still not sure which. But my father was a man who loved his liquor, and by the time he got there he came up with as close an approximation as he was capable at the time.

Which is how I got to be Lucifer Jones.

Anyway, they say that every action has an equal and opposite reaction, and I guess toting the name Lucifer around made me painfully aware of who I was named after. I just naturally kind of gravitated toward the church, especially after I saw the size of our poorbox, and pretty soon me and God formed sort of a two-man company, and I went out and did His business. And a pretty good business it was, until the day a couple of Federal men came around. Up until then I had always thought that paying income taxes was voluntary, like going into the army and such. Well, I'd have stayed and fought them, but the Lord says that vengeance is His, so I took off down the Mississippi one night and hopped the first ship out of New Orleans.

"Well, now," said Rourke when I'd told him the story, adding only a minimum number of poetic flourishes, "I do believe we're going to be friends, Saint Luke. You don't mind if I call you that, do you?"

"It's got a nice, down-to-earth sound to it, Brother Rourke," I allowed. "In fact, now that I roll it around on my tongue, I like it more and more. I think, with your kind permission, that I'll be having these godless black heathen build me the Tabernacle of Saint Luke. Once I leave my present vile surroundings, that is."

"Oh," said Rourke, furrowing up his forehead and tugging at his mustache. "That's too bad. But, of course, if a man's got the call . . ."

"It's a kind of weak call at this moment," I said quickly, wondering what he had in mind. "Nothing that couldn't be fought off for a couple of months if I was to dig in tooth and nail." I gritted my teeth, prepared to make the effort, and he must of mistook it for a grin, because he grinned right back at me.

He unbuttoned his shirt pocket and unfolded a huge sheet of paper. Then he dusted it off a bit and passed it through the bars to me.

"Ever see one of these?" he asked.

I took a quick look and handed it back.

"If it's a map to King Solomon's mines, I've seen about twenty. If it's to the elephants' burial ground, they're kind of rare. I don't imagine I've seen much more than half a dozen in the week I've been here."

He chuckled. "Actually, it's a map to the lost gold mine of the Zulus. Only one I've seen."

"Must have been lost a good long time," I opined. "I don't recall ever seeing a Zulu wearing anything but leopard-claw necklaces."

"Well, what do you think?" asked Rourke.

"About the gold mine?" I asked.

"About the map."

He was still grinning at me, and all of a sudden a great big Heavenly revelation smote me right between the eyes, and out of courtesy I returned his smile.

"How many do you think we could make?" I asked.

"Well, we'd have to hunt up some real old paper, and figure out what kind of charcoal the natives draw with. Need about three bob for materials, I should think."

"You supplied the map, Brother Rourke," I said. "I'll supply the capital. I've got a dozen copies of the Good Book stashed in my hotel room. It shouldn't be too hard to sell them. There's plenty of widows in town who can find solace in the words of Our Lord and His prophets."

"Fine," he said. "I figure we ought to be able to make up about fifty."

"That's a lot of maps," I said. "We wouldn't want to flood the market."

He looked shocked. "That would be immoral. I'm surprised that such a thought would even cross your mind, Saint Luke. Personally, just for propriety's sake, I don't think we should sell more than five an hour."

"At least, not until we get to Pretoria," I agreed.

We consummated our partnership with a solemn handshake.

Burley and I got turned out about a week later, and within another week we had made and sold almost two hundred maps, accumulating a substantial little nest egg along the way.

Of course, the bush was getting a little crowded by then, what with a couple hundred of hopeful investors looking for that lost gold mine, so we swung north to Bechuanaland, where we stopped at an occasional outpost and dispensed maps, medical care, and salvation with equal vigor. I began taking contributions to the Tabernacle of

Saint Luke, and Rourke made a little extra pin money by curing two settlers who didn't have heart attacks and another who hadn't broken his leg. When he came to a trader who really *did* have blackwater fever, he decided that it was time for us to get moving again.

Now, there are a lot of ways for a newly-arrived American and a newly-arrived Irishman to travel through Africa, but foot-slogging ain't one of them. When we weren't pulling scorpions out of our clothes and ticks off our skins, we spent most of our time starving and getting rained on. For what was supposed to be a hot, arid country, I never did see so much rain in all my life. It ruined what was left of the maps, but since we had sold about three hundred by that time, it didn't seem like such a great loss.

Besides, we soon figured out that Zulu gold mines weren't real high on our itinerary, whereas a map to the nearest city would have been a right welcome blessing.

I remember that one night just before our food was due to run out I fell asleep next to an old termite mound. I was still dreaming about an exceptionally nubile daughter of King Solomon, or perhaps it was King David, when Burley kicked me in the ribs. I took the Lord's name in vain a couple of times and tried to go back to sleep, but then he kicked me again.

"Get on your feet, Saint Luke," he said. "We've got company."

I jumped up right quick at that, and peered off in the direction he was looking. There were about twenty half-naked black savages off in the distance, all of them carrying spears and shields.

"Do you reckon they're cannibals, Brother Rourke?" I asked, holding up a hand to shade my eyes from the morning sun.

"Too far away," said Rourke. "I can't see their teeth."

"What have their teeth got to do with it?"

"I read somewhere that all cannibals file their teeth," he said.

I remembered some gossip I had heard about old Doc Peterson back in Moline before they locked him away, and I knew *he* sure didn't file *his* teeth, so I kind of discounted that theory. But they were getting closer now, and most of them looked pretty full, so I figured that it wasn't worth worrying about for the time being.

"What do you think we ought to do?" asked Rourke. "Heal 'em or convert 'em?"

"They don't look like they need much of either," I said, as they approached to within a hundred yards. "I don't suppose you know Zulu or Tswana?"

He shook his head. "They don't speak much of either back in Dublin. How about beads? I'm told they go crazy for beads."

"Sounds reasonable, Brother Rourke," I said. "I didn't know you had any."

"Me? Of course not. Don't you have any rosary beads in your pockets?"

"Wrong religion," I replied.

The savages were about forty yards away now, and muttering amongst themselves. They had slowed down a bit, but were still approaching.

"They look like they mean business," said Rourke. "Suppose we ought to make a run for it?"

"To where?" I asked. "We don't even know where we are."

"The way I figure it," said Rourke, "Cairo's north and the Cape's south. Take your choice."

But by then they had split up, and a moment later we were surrounded. Pulling the Good Book from my pocket, I cleared my throat, raised my hands above my head, and took a step forward.

"*Brethren!*" I shouted, and they all jumped back a couple of steps. "In the Book of Herod, Chapter 8, Verse 3, the Lord God said unto Moses: Thou shall not eat thy neighbor!"

The leader of the heathens stopped dead in his tracks and blinked his eyes very rapidly.

"You're getting to them," said Rourke out of the side of his mouth. "Say something else. Maybe a little hellfire and damnation."

"And the children of Israel were wicked," I intoned. "And you know *why* they were wicked? Because they ate two wayfarers who had mistakenly wandered into their city. For does not Jesus say that to err is human, but to forgive divine? And the children of Israel, who were dressed a far sight better than you, you Godless savages, were cast out into the desert to wander for forty years! Do you want that to happen to you, you ignorant barbarians?"

"Oh, you got 'em on the run, Saint Luke!" said Rourke. "You really got 'em going!"

Well, they got going, all right, but in the wrong direction, and a few seconds later the leader was standing so close to me that I could just about smell his breath.

"Make him smile," said Rourke. "I still want to get a look at his teeth."

The savage responded with an enormous grin. "Like so?" he asked in a deep gravelly voice. Then, frowning, he extended a forefinger and poked me right in the short ribs. "You come!" He jabbed Rourke with the butt of his spear. "You too!"

We acceded to his wishes, not caring to dwell upon the alternatives for any considerable length of time. They didn't treat us unkindly, but then no competent butcher likes to bruise the meat, so I can't say that we were real quick to develop a mutual trust with our black companions. We walked the better part of a day, stopping every now and then for water and privy calls, and when night came we built a big fire and huddled around it, more from cold than from fear of man-eating beasts, of which there weren't none, except maybe for our present company.

Finally the leader walked over to us and sat himself down, cross-legged. He pointed to himself and said, "Kitunga."

"Rourke," said Burley, tapping himself on the chest. "And this here's Saint Luke."

Kitunga solemnly extended his hand, kind of upside down, and shook each of ours.

"Does this mean you're not going to eat us?" asked Rourke.

"Eat you?" said Kitunga, and laughed. "No. No. Not eat."

"Then what do you want from us?" said Rourke.

"*Chumbi-chumbi*," said Kitunga.

"Sounds like some kind of ritual," said Rourke. "What the devil does it mean?"

Kitunga flashed every tooth in his head. "Make babies," he said. He shook our hands again, spat in the fire, and began walking away.

"Hold on a minute!" I said, jumping up. "What do you mean, make babies?"

"Make babies," said Kitunga solemnly. With the forefinger of one hand and the fist of the other, he gave us a graphic and vigorous analogy.

"You mean you want us to make babies with some naked black barbarians?" I demanded.

"Not black," said Kitunga. "Like you."

"You mean a white woman?" asked Rourke.

"Yes, yes," said Kitunga. "White woman."

As you can imagine, we immediately fell to discussing this development between ourselves while Kitunga ambled off to sleep with his men. Back in those days there were lots of tales making the rounds about white women who were priestesses or goddesses of heathen black tribes, but while they sounded good over a lonely campfire or in the bar of the Norfolk Hotel, they were about as likely to be true as our lost Zulu gold mine.

"The way I see it, Brother Rourke," I said after considerable thought, "is that these here savages have killed some hunting party except for a white woman, whom they've doubtless got chained to a post in their village, and whom they probably ravish by the hour."

"I don't know that I'm real pleased about this turn of events, Saint Luke," said Rourke. "Oh, I'll admit that it beats being eaten, but I suppose she's going to want us to rescue her."

It *was* a kind of gloomy thought at that, and I said as much. "Still," I added, "it's the Christian thing to do."

"Maybe you could tell her to turn the other cheek, a fascinating thought in itself," said Rourke.

"Well, I suppose we'd at least better make sure she *wants* to be rescued before we go about upsetting Kitunga," I suggested.

"Right," agreed Rourke. "A person can get used to anything in time. Maybe she's gotten to where she likes being ravished."

"A telling point," I agreed.

We fell silent for a while, and then an interesting notion hit me.

"Brother Rourke," I said, "I think we've been looking at this situation all wrong."

"How so?" he asked.

"Why should a bunch of healthy young bucks want our help ravishing a prisoner?"

"I hadn't quite gotten around to considering that," he admitted. "Now that you mention it, it doesn't really make a lot of sense, does it?"

"It sure as hell don't."

"Scientific curiosity, maybe?" he said.

"Nope," I said. "I been mulling on it for a couple of minutes now, and it seems to me that if they was choosing partners for this white woman, they'd just naturally choose themselves."

"Makes sense," said Rourke, nodding his head thoughtfully.

"Well, then, it stands to reason that if bringing us back with them ain't *their* idea, it must be *hers*."

"Sensible," muttered Rourke. "Sensible."

"And if she's giving orders to a batch of spear-toting heathen like Kitunga and his buddies, she must be a pretty powerful little lady."

"Holy shit!" exclaimed Rourke suddenly. "An oversexed white priestess!" He stared up at the clouds, which were covering up the stars as usual, and got a faraway look on his face. "Golden hair down to her waist," he said, "and breasts like white cantaloupes. Maybe a bracelet or an armband or two . . ."

Well, I couldn't see that the picture he was painting was all that much more enticing than a naked white woman staked out spread-eagled on the ground, but I could tell that Rourke didn't want to be bothered none, so I fell to thinking about what kind of tabernacle me and this white priestess could build right here in the bush before we got around to trading ivory and other such trinkets with civilized folks. I didn't know how big her tribe was, but if Kitunga's group was just a foraging party, I figured we'd have an awful lot of manpower able to respond to a terse command or two. As for Burley, I decided that he wasn't such an all-fired bad fellow, and I'd probably let him stick around as a resident witch doctor, so long as he didn't impose on our hospitality too often, like coming over to dinner of a Sunday or asking us to steal a white woman for him too.

Ten minutes later Rourke was still drawing verbal pictures in the damp night air. By now he'd got her hair down to her ankles, and her breasts were the size of honeydew melons. Seems to me that he'd done away with her armbands, too. He just kept whispering to nobody in particular all night, and by morning he was busy working out the color of her eyes and how narrow her waist was.

Once the sun came up it got warm enough to start traveling again—no matter how hot the days are in Africa, the nights are enough to convince you that you've wandered into Eskimo country by mistake—and Kitunga gave us each a none-too-gentle nudge with the butt of his spear. We began walking, mostly over open veldtland, but occasionally going through sky-high grasses on old elephant and rhino trails, and I fell to questioning him about the white woman.

It didn't help much, since Kitunga had just about run through his entire English vocabulary the day before. I couldn't tell how his tribe had come by this woman, or what she looked like, or if she had been there so long she'd forgotten how to speak in a civilized language, or even why she felt the need to make babies. One thing he did let drop that she was a medicine woman, which was probably as close to being a high priestess as a person could get among these heathen, so Rourke was right on that point at least. I figured it was all to the good, since once she and I started taking field trips to Nairobi and places like that, the tribe would need a good medicine man, and even if Rourke couldn't cure a dysentery germ, he could probably talk it to death.

We walked for two more days. I tried to figure out where we were, but one tree looks pretty much like another, and it was raining so much I never did get a fix on the Southern Cross or any of the constellations, so finally I gave up on it and just followed along. When we bedded down that second night Kitunga gave us to understand, more through gestures than words, that we would reach his village the next morning.

"And that's where we'll meet your witchwoman?" I asked.

"Yes, yes," he said.

"And then we both move in with her?"

"Just one," said Kitunga.

"Just one?" said Rourke, looking a little upset. "What happens to the other?"

Kitunga shrugged and walked away.

"Looks like the winner gets to eat the loser, Brother Rourke," I said at last.

"I'd never eat you, no matter what," said Rourke devoutly.

I fully agreed with that remark, and me and the Lord fell to discussing the matter between ourselves, trying to figure out how best not to present Rourke with any such opportunity.

On the surface of it, there was no problem that I could see, what with me being a handsome and vigorous young stallion, possessed as I was with the eye of a hawk, the heart of a lion, and the gentle hand of a lady. But women are peculiar creatures in matters of taste, and a woman who would send a small battalion of naked warriors out in search of a bed partner was likely to be a little more peculiar than most.

So, having dwelled on the matter for some time, I waited until Rourke was asleep and borrowed a sharp hunting knife from Kitunga. Then I walked to a nearby river, cut off my beard and shaved as close as I could, and washed out all my clothes. On the way back I passed a pile of elephant dung which had been sitting there for some days, picked some up, and carefully smeared it over Rourke's shirt and pants as he slept. I couldn't be sure he'd accept it in the sporting manner in which it was done, so I wandered over to where Kitunga's boys were sleeping and piled in with them. One of them spent half the night grabbing at my ass and giggling, but I awoke whole and in one piece.

Matter of fact, what woke me up was Rourke, screaming at the top of his lungs. He'd flung off all his clothes except for his boots, and was jumping up and down in a right impressive fit of rage. His eyes fell on me, and he pointed an accusing finger in my direction.

"You did it, you Judas!" he screamed. "You son of a bitch! You want her all to yourself! You did it!"

"Calm yourself, Brother Rourke," I said, stepping forward, but still keeping a couple of warriors between him and me. "I don't know quite what you're talking about."

"Damn your hide!" he screamed. "You know bloody well what I'm talking about! Mark my words, you sure as hell aren't going to have her, not without one whopping big fight!"

I just looked at Kitunga and shrugged. He grinned and motioned his men to get moving. "Go now," he said.

"Now just a goddamned minute!" snapped Rourke. "I've got to clean up first."

Kitunga walked over and pointed the business end of his spear at him. "Go now," he said.

Rourke's shoulders sagged. He paused just long enough to transfer his money from his pants pocket into his boot and started walking off with us. He made a pretty comical picture walking through the bush, six and a half feet tall, skinny as a rail, and wearing nothing but his beat-up old hunting boots, but I thought it safer to admire him from afar and always kept half a dozen men between us.

In about two hours we reached the top of a hill, and, looking down, I could see a batch of thorn huts sitting beside a stream that ran through a large valley.

I adjusted my jacket, buttoned my shirt up to the collar, tried to comb my hair a bit with my fingers, and turned to Kitunga.

"What's her name?" I asked.

"Neeyora," he said.

It had a lovely lilt to it, just the kind of name that ought to go with being a gorgeous priestess among these godless savages, and I started marching down the hill to the valley so as not to prolong Rourke's agony any more than was strictly necessary.

When I got within about a hundred yards of the village I stopped right sudden-like and blinked my eyes once or twice. Then I looked ahead again to make sure it was no mirage.

"Brother Rourke," I said. He stopped in his tracks and just glared at me without answering. "I done a terrible thing this morning, a wickedly sinful thing, and I want to make amends. If you'd like my clothes, all except for my hat which I need to shield me from the heat and the rain, I'll gladly turn them over to you right now."

"What the hell are you talking about?" said Rourke, a totally unwarranted look of suspicion on his face.

"I just don't want the Lord looking down with displeasure on me for trying to trick you like I did," I said.

I started unbuttoning my shirt, but Kitunga pointed his spear right at the middle of my belly and, smiling like all get-out, shook his head vigorously.

"But I just want to give him something to wear," I said.

"No, no," he said, prodding my belly with the point of his spear blade.

"What's this all about?" demanded Rourke, walking over.

"You were right about her being blonde," I said. "But you were a little on the conservative side about her breasts."

"What do you mean?" said Rourke, looking suspicious.

"Not honeydew melons, Brother Rourke," I said with a sigh. "Watermelons."

He shaded his eyes and looked toward the village. There, sitting in front of the largest hut, was our half-naked white priestess. More to the point, she was about ninety-five percent naked; it would have taken the hide of a small elephant to cover half of her.

Her hair was blonde under the dirt and the grease. Even as we approached I couldn't tell what color her eyes were; they were sunken too far beneath the folds of flab to even tell if she had any. Her shoulder spread would have done a bull gorilla proud, and her breasts, which sagged down well below her waist, could have given sustenance to an army. She was sitting in the mud, rolling bones and the dried-out carcasses of small lizards on the ground in front of her. It looked like she was trying to sit cross-legged, but her legs were too fat to bend. Rourke had been wrong about the bracelet too. I don't think they could have made one big enough to fit her.

"*That?*" gasped Rourke. "That's Neeyora?"

Kitunga nodded.

Rourke turned to me, grinning. "I don't know how to thank you, Saint Luke!" His eyes darted over the ground. "You don't see any more elephant shit, do you?" Then he began laughing and threw a dung-covered arm around my shoulders. "We'll let bygones be bygones!" he said, and began walking up to Neeyora's hut.

"Father, why hast Thou forsaken me?" I muttered, and allowed myself to be led into the village.

Neeyora looked up, and if she was less than desirable in repose, she was absolutely mind-boggling in animation. She grinned from ear to ear, a pretty fair distance given the size of her face, said something I couldn't understand to Kitunga, and began licking her lips. Two of the villagers helped her slowly to her feet, and she approached us, giggling like a crazy woman. Her tiny little eyes—now that I was close enough, I could see that they were red—darted from one of us to the other. She reached out and pinched my upper arm, and Rourke just stood there, laughing like a lunatic.

Then she walked over to the Irishman, who was every bit as dirty and foul-smelling and naked as she was, and it was love at first sight. She gave a jubilant little scream, threw her arms around him—which practically made the bottom three-quarters of him vanish from sight—and began dragging him off to her hut.

"Don't just stand there, Luke!" hollered Rourke. "Do something! "

If I'd had my mouth organ with me I suppose I could have played "Here Comes the Bride," but under the current circumstances I thought it best to keep a low profile, so other than offering Brother Rourke a few appropriate quotes on love and marriage from the Good Book, I just smiled and waved goodbye to him as he vanished into the darkened recesses of his bridal bower. A high-pitched shriek a couple of minutes later gave me to understand that he had also vanished into the darkened recesses of his bride.

Well, Kitunga and I and the boys wandered over to one of the huts and started drinking some home-brewed beer and swapping tall stories. I didn't understand a word they said, and I don't imagine they understood me either, but what with the beer and all we became pretty fast friends by the time Rourke staggered out of his hut a couple of hours later. I don't think Job at his lowest could have looked any worse.

All the fire had gone out of his eyes, and he looked kind of shrunken. He collapsed next to me, and I handed him a cup of native brew. He drank it without a word.

I turned to Kitunga. "Now that he's made the babies, can we go?"

That tickled Kitunga's funny bone for some reason, and he emitted a roar of laughter.

This was a little unsettling, for I still didn't know exactly what happened to unsuccessful suitors. Rourke looked like he wouldn't have the energy to leave anyway, so I decided to let the subject drop for the moment.

We sat there swigging beer and singing songs for a little while longer, and then I heard a deep voice bellow: "*Rerrk!*"

"Oh, God, not again!" muttered Rourke.

"*Rerrk!*" hollered Neeyora, sounding just a little louder than a bull elephant in *musth*.

Rourke reached into his boot and pulled out his share of our money, which was about three hundred British pounds.

"Take it," he said. "It's all yours. If you ever get back to civilization . . ."

"I'll organize a party and come back here for you," I promised, crossing a couple of fingers behind my back.

He laughed weakly. "I'll never last that long. No, what I want you to do is buy a headstone for me and plant it in the graveyard at Johannesburg. If there's any money left"—I assured him there would be, and made a solemn vow to see to it—"walk into the nearest bar and buy a round for everyone in the house and drink to my memory."

"You sure you wouldn't rather have your name engraved on a pew in my tabernacle?" I asked thoughtfully.

"Just do what I said," whispered Rourke.

"*Rerrk!*"

Two of Kitunga's men helped Rourke to his feet and led him back to his blushing bride.

While he was gone, the rest of us got down to serious drinking. I quietly suggested to the Lord that now might be an admirable time for Him to give me the strength of ten men because my heart was pure, and sure enough, I was the only one who didn't pass out in the next hour. I quietly filled my canteen with one last batch of brew and walked on out of the village just as free as a bird.

When I reached the top of the hill I paused to take one last look, partly out of sentiment but mostly to make sure that no one was pursuing me yet. There wasn't a sign of life in the whole village. Then I saw a figure crawl out of a hut and start making toward the beer, and a few seconds later I heard a truly ear-splitting scream of "*RERRK!*"

And that was the last I ever saw of Burley Rourke and his white priestess.

2. PARTNERS

I wandered north and east, fell in for a while with a Canadian named Pinder who was single-handedly drinking his way from the Cape to Cairo, made it to the railhead in Uganda, and took the train all the way to Mombasa on the coast, where I had the bad fortune to run into three different parties I had sold maps to. They failed totally to see the humor in the situation or to realize that their donations had gone to a worthy cause, and discretion being the better part of valor, I took a vigorous stroll to the south and wound up in Dar-es-Salaam, which was the capital of Tanganyika.

Dar-es-Salaam wasn't like any other town in British East. It was on the ocean, but wasn't much of a seaport; it was in Africa, but there was nothing bigger or more ferocious than a goat within thirty miles; it was a capital, but it couldn't have held six buildings that could resist a strong wind. It was composed, in almost equal parts, of East Indians, black Africans, and reprobates from all over the world.

I felt right at home.

I took a room at the only hotel in town, shaved and showered, had a big dinner, and went to Maurice's, a bar down by the waterfront. Sometime around midnight I found myself in the back room, betting on scorpion races, and the Lord being on my side, I wound up the night with about two thousand pounds in winnings.

When I returned to my room I found a man sitting down on one of the chairs there. He was tall, though nowhere near as tall as Rourke, with piercing gray eyes and a neatly trimmed little goatee. He was dressed all in black: hat, shirt, tie, vest, jacket, belt, pants, socks, shoes. In point of fact, he made my preaching clothes look like an outfit of gossamer gaiety.

"Begging your pardon, brother," I said, "but ain't you in the wrong room?"

"I hardly think so," he said in a voice so slick and cultured you could have used it for cooking oil. "Allow me to introduce myself. My name is Dobbins, Major Theodore Dobbins, late of His Majesty's armed forces." He handed me his card, which was just a little frayed around the edges, and was black with white lettering on it.

I extended my hand. "The Right Reverend Doctor Jones at your service," I said.

"Well, my dear Doctor Jones," he said, pulling out a cigarette and putting it into a mother-of-pearl holder, "I shan't beat about the bush. I have come to you because I am in need of your help."

"I'm always happy to help a soul in need, Major," I said, sitting down on the edge of the bed. "Of course, you understand that spiritual aid and comfort does get a little expensive at this time of night."

"It is not spiritual aid that I seek, sir," he said with a dry chuckle. "Indeed it is not. I am given to understand that you came into possession of a considerable amount of money earlier this evening. Is this not correct?"

"The Good Lord saw fit to smile upon me," I admitted.

"Excellent!" He was positively beaming now while puffing away at his cigarette. "Then I am in the position to suggest a brief alliance which may work to our mutual benefit, involving as it does a pooling of resources."

"This money is being held in escrow for the Tabernacle of Saint Luke," I replied with dignity. Then I thought about it, and added, "However, to be perfectly honest, construction ain't due to begin for another few months when the rainy season ends, and I imagine my parishioners wouldn't be averse to an extremely conservative short-term investment."

"I understand perfectly, my dear sir," he said with a smile. Even his teeth looked oily. "I deal in commodities, Doctor Jones. Many of these are in the form of highly perishable goods imported from the fields of far, exotic China. Such a shipment is currently aboard a vessel anchored not five hundred yards from us." He paused to light another cigarette. "May I presume that you fully comprehend my position?"

"I think we're on the same wave length," I allowed.

"Well, then, you can imagine my dismay when I discovered that my associate, who was on his way here from Marrakech, was waylaid and murdered by a band of Arab slave traders. My goods are in the harbor, my principals await their delivery in the Mediterranean, my caravan has been hired, yet I am temporarily unable to set the wheels of industry in motion. The entire enterprise has ground to a halt for lack of the necessary capital. Worse yet, my competitors, knowing that something has gone amiss, are waiting like jackals at the kill. In brief, sir, I must have no less than seventeen hundred British pounds. The return on your investment, within a mere matter of days, will be tenfold."

"What's the nature of your competition?" I asked.

He waved a hand vaguely, as if shooing a fly away. "Men of little breeding and less ethics. Hardly worthy of notice, except for this unfortunate turn of affairs. One of them is actually a trafficker in human flesh."

"Not God-fearing gentlemen like us?"

"My dear Doctor Jones!" he said, shaking my hand warmly. "We understand one another completely! May I assume that we are partners?"

"I'll have to spend the night in prayer, conferring with the Lord and getting His advice on the subject," I said. "Suppose I meet you for dinner at Maurice's tomorrow night and give you my decision at that time."

"Certainly," he said, rising and walking to the door. Just before he left, he turned and said, "Remember, my dear sir, that God helps those who help themselves."

"That sentiment ain't never far from my mind," I assured him.

After he left, I settled down to thinking seriously about the Major's proposal. I felt certain that, understanding my goals as He did, the Lord wouldn't mind my entering into this little enterprise. Just the same, as my Silent Partner, I knew that He'd want me to look into all aspects of it very carefully. For example, it stood to reason that if the goods were still aboard the ship, the Major's competition also lacked the necessary funding, and while a thousand percent profit was a healthy return on my investment, I could build my tabernacle a lot quicker with a two thousand percent return. Therefore, just before I fell asleep, I made up my mind to see if I couldn't hunt up the Major's rivals.

As it turned out, I didn't have to do much in the way of hunting at all. I was sitting at my table on the hotel's veranda the next morning, drinking my coffee and waiting for some ostrich eggs and toast, when a stout gentleman dressed in a soiled white suit walked up and seated himself opposite me. His hair was so thin that his skull shone through in half a hundred places, all red and covered with sweat which ran down his face in little rivulets until it got caught up in his beard.

"Doctor Jones?" he said, pulling out a handkerchief and mopping his forehead. He had an accent I couldn't quite place.

"The Right Reverend Doctor Jones," I acknowledged, sipping my coffee.

"It has come to my attention that you had a visitor last night."

"I've nothing to hide, brother," I said. "I met with Major Theodore Dobbins, late of His Majesty's armed forces."

He laughed. "Until he was court-martialed for embezzling," he said. "I assume he put forth a proposition to you?"

"That he did."

His eyes narrowed slightly. "I hope you were not so impetuous as to enter into any business agreement with him."

"Cautious is my middle name, brother," I said. "I'm still mulling over his offer."

"Good!" he said. "You had a very narrow escape, Doctor Jones. You cannot begin to know the nature of the man with whom you were speaking."

"True," I agreed. "On the other hand, I *do* know his name."

"Forgive me," he said, wiping his head again. "I am known as the Dutchman."

"Just the Dutchman?"

He nodded. "I do have a large variety of business names," he added helpfully, "if using one of them would make you more comfortable."

"Not at all," I said, pouring another cup of coffee. Then I looked up at him quickly. "You wouldn't happen to be a slave trader, would you?"

He sat up erect and said, "I prefer to think of myself as the director of an international occupational placement service."

I signaled to the waiter. "Won't you join me for breakfast, Dutchman? I have a feeling that we've got a lot to talk about."

"Just coffee, thank you," he said. The waiter brought a large pot and left it on the table. The Dutchman poured himself half a cup, waved away my offer of cream and sugar, and withdrew a small flask from his coat pocket, pouring a generous amount into the cup and stirring it vigorously.

"Doctor Jones," he said after taking a man-sized swallow and screwing up his face, "may I speak frankly with you?"

"Well, it might make a pleasant change," I answered.

"I am in need of a certain amount of venture capital: fourteen hundred pounds, to be exact. You won considerably more than that last night. I would like to arrange a short-term loan."

"Have you considered a bank?" I asked.

"Yes, I have," he replied. "But the bank at Dar-es-Salaam is well fortified, and would be most difficult to break into."

"I assume that your credit rating would make a more forthright approach out of the question?"

He nodded vigorously. "There must be a prejudice against Hollanders in Tanganyika. I can conceive of no other reason for it. At any rate, will you consider such a transaction?"

"Jesus only threw the money-lenders out of the Temple," I said with a smile. "I don't recall the Good Book making any reference to throwing them out of Dar-es-Salaam."

"Then may I assume that we have a deal?" said the Dutchman.

"Well, now, that's putting the cart just a little bit ahead of the horse," I said. "What interest would you be expecting to pay?"

"Shall we say one thousand percent for ten days?"

"Well, that's a right round number," I said. "All them zeroes and everything. A very pretty number indeed."

"Good!" exclaimed the Dutchman. "Shall we draw up a contract right away?"

"Of course, fifteen hundred is just as pretty," I continued. "I think there ought to be a five in there somewhere. Always liked fives, ever since I was a toddler. And I suppose two zeroes is just as good as three. Reminds me more of one of Solomon's wives that way."

"Such a figure is out of the question!" snapped the Dutchman. "I know that our mutual friend couldn't have offered you that much."

"What he offered me, Dutchman," I said, "is a matter known only to him, me, and the Lord."

"I shall have to speak to my investors," said the Dutchman.

"That's perfectly understandable," I replied. "I think a short session of prayer might help you to come to a decision."

"I will meet again with you tonight," he said, finishing his coffee and rising.

"I'll be at Maurice's most of the evening," I said. "I'm meeting Major Dobbins there for dinner."

"Make no commitment until you hear from me," said the Dutchman. "And remember that I sell merchandise of *all* colors."

Well, I didn't know if that was a threat or an offer, so I just smiled at him and watched him waddle away. Then I dug into breakfast with a vengeance, after which I walked to the harbor. I figured the goods would be in a rust-covered seedy-looking scow, but there were so many of them there that I knew right away that I'd never be able to spot the one that had brought Saint Luke's Tabernacle this little windfall.

As I was walking back to my hotel I noticed a small, olive-colored man following me. He was sneaking in and out of shadows just like a real-life spy, except that he was so clumsy about it that he damned near went through a couple of plate-glass windows trying to jump out of my line of vision. Just to make certain it was me he was after, I took a walk through the Arab quarter, and sure enough, he was still about two hundred feet behind me half an hour later.

It being a hot day and the air being as thick as salt water, I finally took pity on him, turned in my tracks, and walked right up to him. As I approached, he looked so scared that I thought he was going to faint dead away, but he settled for gulping twice and sweating a lot.

"Good afternoon, brother," I said cheerfully. "Would it be easier on you if I just found a nice shady bench and sat down on it?"

He nodded.

"Cat got your tongue?" I asked.

"Most assuredly not," he said in a high nasal voice. "Or is that an American colloquialism?"

"No, it's just slang," I said. "Let's rid ourselves of the formalities. The Right Reverend Doctor Jones at your service." I extended my hand, and he looked so startled that I thought he was going to jump clear up to the moon.

"And I am Henri Pasquard," he said when he'd stopped shaking.

"Can't say that I've ever heard of you, brother," I said.

"Oh, nobody has," he said solemnly. "That is essential to my business. But possibly you have heard of Le Rongeur?"

"Nope."

He looked disappointed.

"What does it mean?" I asked.

"Oh, nothing much. It's just my professional name, sort of like a stage name for an actor."

I was about to pat him on the shoulder and tell him not to look so unhappy, but I didn't want him to start shaking again, so I settled for offering him a cigar.

"Oh, I don't smoke," he said. "The smell makes me ill."

"Then I won't inflict the stench of my tobacco on you," I said, putting the one I had chosen for myself back into my pocket. His hair was all slicked down with grease, and the grease and sweat were starting to run down his forehead into his eyes, so I offered him a handkerchief. He accepted it with a brief murmur of thanks.

"Would you care to tell me why you were following me, Brother Rongeur?" I said, hoping the use of his professional name would put him more at ease.

"I meant to approach you sooner or later," he said, staring down at his two-toned shoes, "but is it not reasonable that I should first see if I could determine where you might have hidden the money?"

"Reasonable as all get-out," I agreed. "And now that you know it's not on me and that I'm not going to lead you to it, what next?"

"Why, I should like to propose a partnership, of course," he said. "Major Dobbins is a thief of the lowest type, and the Dutchman is even worse. I should think that dealing with such people would be repugnant to a man of your character."

"Whereas dealing with a man like yourself . . . ?"

"Please do not think that I offer you only honesty and integrity," he said quickly. "On the contrary, I will return your money threefold in a week's time."

"I've already had better offers than that," I said.

"I have no doubt of it," said the little man, almost apologetically. "But what good are their offers once they have their hands on the material? I, without false modesty, can give you a list of references which will satisfy even a man of the cloth. I can—" He broke off suddenly. "Excuse me," he said, withdrawing an impressive-looking pistol from a shoulder holster and tucking it into his belt. "I tend to sweat under my arms, and moisture ruins the mechanism. Where were we?"

"I believe you were about to list your references," I said.

"That would perhaps be indiscreet, until such time as I know you are interested in a partnership," he said.

"Perfectly understandable," I said. "Just out of curiosity, Brother Rongeur, what exactly do you do when you're not striking up partnerships?"

"Oh, I try to keep busy at one thing or another," he said, lowering his eyes again.

"And what does Le Rongeur mean?"

"The Rodent," he said, blushing under his olive skin. "Originally I was the Weasel, but there is no masculine form of it in French. It is always La Belette. It became very embarrassing, and attracted an inferior sort of person, if you understand my meaning."

"But why rodent or weasel or any kind of animal at all?" I asked.

"It's kind of a private joke," he said, still blushing furiously.

"Care to let me in on it, Brother Rongeur?"

"Then it wouldn't be private any longer, would it?" he replied. "Besides, it really has very little to do with the business at hand. Have you reached a decision?"

"I'll have to spend some time weighing all my offers very carefully," I said. "I should be able to come to a decision by tonight. I can meet you at—"

"Oh, we needn't make any arrangements, Doctor Jones," he interrupted. "I don't intend to let you out of my sight for the rest of the day."

"Oh?"

"I don't mean to disturb you, but you must understand my position. Just go on about your business as if I weren't here. I shall try to be as unobtrusive as possible."

I thanked him and began walking back to the hotel. Every now and again I'd turn back and, sure enough, there he'd be, ducking in and out of shadows about fifty feet behind me. He was such a skinny little man and I got to feeling so sorry for him that once or twice, when I got too far ahead of him, I'd browse at a vendor's table and give him a chance to catch up, for which he shot me a couple of very grateful smiles.

I finally got to my room, relaxed in the cast-iron tub for an hour, shaved, and lay down for a little nap. When I woke up it was getting on toward sunset, so I changed into my Sunday preaching clothes and decided it was time to stroll over to Maurice's. The Rodent was waiting for me on the hotel veranda, and began following me at a respectful distance.

Maurice's was exotic and dirty, with about a three-to-one ratio in favor of the dirt. There were a number of rooms with pretty far-fetched doorframes, all separated by rows of hanging beads. The lighting throughout the place was dim, the air was circulated by a couple of very large and slow-turning overhead fans, and the walls were covered with animal heads, tapestries, and paintings of very naked ladies. I paused in the bar just long enough to stuff a couple of bills in the brassiere of a belly dancer and then walked into one of the smaller back rooms, where I found Major Dobbins, late of His Majesty's armed forces, sitting at a table and puffing away at his cigarette holder.

"Ah!" he exclaimed as his gaze fell upon me. "My dear Doctor Jones! I trust your day went well."

"So far, so good," I assured him. "Of course, it ain't over yet."

"True," he said, his eyes twinkling. "But any day that begins with a visit from the Dutchman can't fail but to get better, eh?" He chortled and poured half a flask of gin into his water glass. Then, stirring it up a little with a dirty coffee spoon, he drank it down in a single swallow. "I know it irritates Maurice," he confided, "but I simply cannot tolerate his bar stock. And as for his wine cellar..." He gave a man-of-the-world shrug, and I nodded in my most sophisticated manner.

At this moment the Rodent walked into our room and sat down at an adjoining table. He gave us a nervous little smile and immediately buried his nose in the menu, which was kind of strange since the only thing Maurice ever served was impala steak.

"You know him, I presume?" said the Major, nodding in the Rodent's direction.

"Met him this afternoon," I said.

"He made you an offer?"

"He did."

"You turned him down, naturally," said the Major.

"Why naturally?"

"Anyone could tell just by looking at him that he's a man of weak moral character," said the Major. "Hardly the kind of person you'd care to enter into business with. See how he keeps peeking at us over the top of his menu. No, my dear sir, we Englishmen have to stick together."

"I'm an American," I pointed out.

"Same thing," he said. "Shall we get down to details now?"

At just that moment the Dutchman walked in and came over to our table. "I'm sure you don't mind if I join you," he said, pulling up a chair. He had a different white suit on, but it was, if anything, even more soiled than the last one.

"Personally, I have no objections whatsoever," said the Major. "However, my good friend Doctor Jones is in a hurry to conclude our business. It might be best if you returned in an hour or so."

The Dutchman cracked his knuckles and sank even deeper into the tiny wooden chair. "My friend Doctor Jones seems to have fallen into a pit of vipers," he said at last. "Once I extricate him, he will know who his real friends are." He paused to light a very bent cigarette. "By the way, what is Le Rongeur doing at the next table?"

"I am trying to decide what to order," said the little man with some haughtiness.

"Well, that takes care of *him* for the next forty-five minutes," said the Dutchman. "What has this phony offered you, Doctor Jones?" he said, jerking a thumb in the Major's face.

I thought the Major might take a swing at him, but instead he just laughed jovially and turned to me. "You've spoken to both of us, my good sir," he said. "I put it to you: Which of us is the more trustworthy?"

I looked from one to the other, and to tell the truth, I had considerable difficulty making up my mind. Then, suddenly, the Rodent hissed between his teeth, and all eyes turned to the doorway, through which stepped a tall, well-groomed white man wearing a police uniform.

"Well, well, what have we here?" he said with a smile. "I really should get a photograph of this, and title it *Thieves' Carnival*." He turned to me. "You wouldn't happen to be Lucifer Jones, would you?"

"The Right Reverend Doctor Jones," I replied.

"I thought as much," he said. "I am Captain Peter Clarke, at your service, sir—and the biggest service I can offer you is to urge you not to enter into any transactions with your current companions."

"What makes you think I was considering such a thing, Brother Clarke?" I asked.

"When you're out in the bush and you see vultures circling in the sky, what makes you think there's a carcass on the ground?" he replied with a smile. "I assure you, Doctor Jones, that the mere presence of these three swindlers is ample proof to anyone who knows them that you are in possession of a tidy piece of change. I can only urge you to hang on to it for dear life."

"I did not come here to have my character impugned," said the Major.

"I can do more than impugn it," laughed Captain Clarke. "I can document it. Major Theodore Dobbins, age forty-six, dishonorably discharged for embezzlement, served three terms for fraud in England, one for robbery in Australia. Currently on probation from Johannesburg. Wanted in Ethiopia, Morocco, and Egypt for drug dealing."

He turned to the Dutchman. "And this one's another treasure: Caesare Tobur, alias Winston Riles, alias Hans Gerber, alias Horst Brokow, alias the Dutchman. Wanted in seven countries for slave trading and in three more for the illegal sale of firearms."

"Then why haven't you arrested them?" I asked, more out of politeness than a fervent desire to see any potential meal tickets locked away.

"Inefficient extradition laws," said Captain Clarke. "Tanganyika was a German protectorate until a few years ago. It still takes an enormous amount of paperwork to get things done here. Besides, we don't know which ship is carrying the opium, but we do know that someone is going to have to make a move in the next day or so. I hope you'll forgive my frankness, Doctor Jones, but I'd hate to see you get mixed up with these characters. And that little weasel sitting at the next table is the worst of the lot."

"I beg your pardon!" said the Rodent, rising to his feet.

"Worst butcher in all of British East," said Captain Clarke. "He's killed something like thirty-five men."

"That's a lie!" screamed the Rodent. He turned to me. "I put it to you, my dear friend. I have killed only sixteen men, all in self-defense. I have never been convicted of murder. There are no warrants for my arrest anywhere in Africa. And yet this . . . this *fou* tries to make me sound like a mad-dog killer. Me, Le Rongeur, who wouldn't harm a fly unless provoked!" He sneered at Clarke. "Thirty-five men indeed!"

"Well, what do you say, Doctor Jones?" said Captain Clarke. "Would you care to have me escort you back to your hotel, or possibly put you into protective custody until the deadline for the deal has passed?"

"I thank you for your concern, Brother Clarke," I said, "but surrounded as I am by the scum of the earth, what better place could I find to do the Lord's bidding? Why don't you check back in on me in a couple of hours?"

"If you're still alive," said Clarke grimly.

"I'll have 'em singing hosannahs in half that time," I said with a confident smile.

"Well, I can't *force* you to use your brain," said Captain Clarke with a shrug. He turned and left the room.

"I hope you will accept what he said with a grain of salt," said the Major.

"Obviously misinformed," said the Dutchman.

"I wonder who killed the other nineteen men?" mused the Rodent.

A waiter approached us just then, and we all ordered impala, except the Rodent, who insisted on having fish. The waiter, after some argument, finally agreed, provided that the Rodent wouldn't object if his fish looked and tasted like impala. The little man finally nodded, the waiter left, and I was alone with my confederates once again.

"As I was saying," began the Major, "you must by now realize what kind of social untouchables have joined us in our repast. We have a demented dwarf who can't remember how many men he's killed, and a slave trader called the Dutchman who's probably never been within two hundred miles of Holland."

"Hah!" snapped the Dutchman. "I grew up in Rakovnik!"

"Which happens to be in Czechoslovakia," said the Rodent softly from the next table.

"Amsterdam!" amended the Dutchman quickly. "I grew up in Amsterdam. It's been such a long time that I get confused."

"And what about yourself, Major?" I asked. "Did you really serve time in all those prisons?"

"A series of unfortunate misunderstandings," he said smoothly. "But let us come back to the point, sir. I have made you a very generous proposition. Are we to be partners?"

"And I have made him an even better one!" said the Dutchman.

"At any rate," said the Major. "I feel certain that we may at least eliminate Le Rongeur from consideration. You cannot possibly entertain the notion of entering into an agreement with such a man."

As the Major finished speaking, the Rodent made a sudden move with his right hand, and I found myself alone at the table, both my companions having dropped to the floor with a swiftness born of terror. The Rodent merely smiled, picked his napkin from his lap, and dabbed himself about the lips.

"That was a thoroughly uncivil thing to do," complained the Major, getting back onto his chair.

"You would prefer that I let my wine trickle down my chin?" asked the Rodent gently.

"We would prefer that you not make any sudden movements in the direction of your belt," said the Dutchman, huffing and puffing as he regained his feet.

"My apologies, gentlemen," said the Rodent. "Next time I feel the need to reach for anything below the line of your vision, I shall first announce what I am reaching for."

The Major nodded vigorously. "It's only good manners."

"I must add," said the Rodent, "that if you make any further attempt to convince my good friend Doctor Jones that I am unable to fulfill my word as an independent businessman, the next thing I reach for will not be my napkin. I wish you no ill will, but . . ." He let the sentence die with an apologetic little smile.

"Back to business," said the Dutchman. "Doctor Jones, I am prepared to offer you double anything the Major offers."

"Rubbish!" said the Major. "I'll match whatever that gross peddler of human flesh offers. We Englishmen must stick together."

"And you, Rongeur?" I asked, turning to the little man. "What do you have to say?"

"My offer is unchanged since this morning," said the Rodent. "But there is one thing I must add to it."

"Please do so," I said.

"I am willing to guarantee that none of my rivals will take, shall we say, unsavory means to show you his displeasure at not becoming your partner. I do not think they can make the same guarantee."

I must confess that it was a contract stipulation that hadn't occurred to me, and the more I thought about it, the better the Rodent's offer began to look. Founding the Tabernacle of Saint Luke was all well and good, but not if the founder was to be buried beneath a cornerstone. I suppose I wasn't upholding my poker face very well, because the Major laid a reassuring hand on my shoulder.

"My dear Doctor Jones," he said, "I assure you that my principals will not allow any harm to come to you, if that's all that is worrying you."

"I make you the same guarantee," said the Dutchman, "with the further stipulation that should my guarantee not, for some unforeseen reason, be fulfilled, you will be brutally and thoroughly avenged."

"Brother Dutchman," I said, "as much as I appreciate the sentiments behind your statement, I find it a mighty small comfort. Let us leave such dismal considerations aside for the moment and start talking cold hard cash."

"Excellent," said the Dutchman. "You know my terms. I will give you a thousand percent return within ten days."

"How will I find you ten days from now?" I asked.

"You might ask the local constabulary," said the Major nastily. "He spends more time in jail than out of it."

"You are hardly the one to make such a statement!" said the Dutchman haughtily.

"Brethren," I said, "I repeat: My prime concern is making sure that I have some way of collecting all these wondrous profits that are being spoken of. I couldn't love and trust you more if you were my own flesh and blood—but then, my own flesh-and-blood brother is currently serving time in Arizona for trying to rob a restaurant. Therefore, I feel that I need more than verbal assurances, no matter how comforting they may be." (Actually, my brother was in jail in Montana for doing vile things with a painted woman and her twelve-year-old twin daughters, but I saw no reason to bring his sordid misdeeds to light just to prove a point.)

"I appreciate your concern, my dear sir," said the Major, "but you must understand that time is of the essence. If the money is not presented by noon tomorrow, the boat will leave for Madagascar, where the goods will be offered to Erich Von Horst."

"And who is this Von Horst?" I asked.

"A black-hearted scoundrel," said the Dutchman. "A totally unprincipled swine."

"But smart," interposed the Rodent.

"Yes, smart," said the Dutchman. "No one even knows what he looks like, or if Von Horst is his real name. But he has made enormous inroads on this segment of our business."

"In other words," I said, "he is a competitor."

"An understatement," said the Major. "The man is a monopolist. Far from being a competitor, he tries to beat down competition at every opportunity. In short, he is an enemy of the free-enterprise system."

"Well, brothers," I said, "I certainly agree that we can't allow a man like that to blacken his soul still further. He sounds like he's pretty nearly past redemption right now, and I've certainly got no intention of helping old Satan get his infernal claws on another brother through any action of mine. No, indeed, we certainly can't be the cause of poor Brother Von Horst's downfall."

"Excellent, my dear Doctor Jones," said the Major. "We shall at least, so to speak, keep it within the family. Now, with whom do you choose to associate yourself?"

"Brothers," I said, "I know I said I would announce my decision at dinner tonight, but certain factors have been brought to light by our frank discussion. If each of you will meet me for breakfast at my hotel tomorrow morning and tell me how you intend to protect both my investment and my health, I will choose one of you in ample time for you to purchase your goods before noon." I paused to borrow a swig of the Major's liquor. "You understand that it's not myself I'm concerned about. But to rob me is to rob the Lord of His tabernacle, and that is just too sinful to contemplate."

Well, none of them looked too happy about it, but I guess they all saw the wisdom of my position, for they finally agreed, though the Rodent kept playing with his napkin and shooting regretful but meaningful glances at the Major and the Dutchman.

We kept drinking and talking about one thing and another for an hour or so, and then Captain Peter Clarke came back in. I hadn't wanted to offend any of my friends, but the truth of the matter is that I had been waiting for him, just to make sure I got back to the hotel safe and sound, so bidding them all adieu until morning, I began walking back to my hotel in his company.

"How'd you make out with that pack of thieves?" said Captain Clarke. "Still got your wallet?"

"So far so good, Brother Clarke," I said. "But there is something I've been meaning to discuss with you." I turned quickly and saw three different but distinctive figures darting in and out amongst the shadows.

"And what might that be, Doctor Jones?" asked Captain Clarke.

"I have a certain amount of cash on hand," I said.

"I know," said Captain Clarke.

"And being a God-fearing and moral man, I would never harm my fellow man, so I carry no weapons. Now, you made a statement earlier this evening about protective custody..."

"True," he said. "But the situation has changed in the past hour. Our prison has only four cells, and thanks to a drunken brawl at the waterfront, I regret to inform you that all four of our accommodations are currently occupied."

"I wasn't referring to myself, Brother Clarke," I said quickly. "As a man of the cloth, I have naturally never spent so much as a minute in a jail cell, and I think such an experience would be spiritually shattering."

"Then what did you have in mind, Doctor Jones?" he said.

"I have a certain amount of cash on hand," I began.

"So you said."

"I wonder if I might put it in protective custody until, shall we say, ten o'clock tomorrow morning?"

"Well, it's highly irregular..." he said.

"I'd rest much easier knowing it's free from attack by vicious night-prowling bandits and other foul denizens of the city," I said.

"You'd pick it up no later than ten o'clock?" said Captain Clarke.

"My word as a man of God," I said, raising my right hand and shooting a glance up toward Heaven.

"And you're willing to trust me?"

"You're a sworn defender of the law, ain't you?" I said.

"All right, Doctor Jones," he said. "If this is truly your desire, I suppose the city of Dar-es-Salaam can keep your money in custody overnight. Where is it?"

"I'll lead you to it," I said, "just as soon as we manage to elude my dinner companions."

"Oh, so you noticed them too?" he said with a smile. "It shouldn't be too difficult to get rid of them."

We speeded up our pace and began turning this way and that, and within half an hour even the Rodent must have been wondering where we had gone to. Then we doubled back to Maurice's, where we crept around to the back of the building and I removed my money from beneath a large concrete block where I had hidden it the night before.

Captain Clarke counted it briskly, then put it in his pocket and withdrew a pencil and a small notebook.

"Let me give you a receipt for it," he said, and scrawled laboriously that the Police Department of the city of Dar-es- Salaam owed the Right Reverend Doctor Lucifer Jones the sum of two thousand and forty British pounds, payable upon presentation of this note.

"All nice and official," he said, signing his name with a flourish. "See you tomorrow morning, Doctor Jones."

I made my way back to the hotel, where I found Major Dobbins, the Dutchman, and the Rodent waiting for me in the lobby. I bade them all goodnight, and went up to my room.

I was awakened by a pounding at the door. I looked out the window and saw that it was still dark. Using the Lord's name for purposes other than it was intended, I pulled on my pants and walked across the room. When I opened the door all three of them practically fell through it.

"Gentlemen!" I said harshly. "I thought we were to meet at breakfast."

"Quickly!" said the Major. "What have you done with the money?"

"I hardly consider that a proper request," I said, pushing my hair back out of my eyes.

The Rodent pulled out his pistol and pushed it into my belly. "Where is the money?" he shrieked.

"Brothers," I said, "I am truly shocked. I thought we had an understanding."

"The money!" screamed the Rodent. "Who did you give it to?"

"To Captain Peter Clarke of the Dar-es-Salaam police force," I replied angrily. "It'll be kept there in safety and security until I make my decision. Although," I added, "based on this unwarranted intrusion, I wonder if the Lord would wish me to enter into financial dealings with any of you."

"Fool!" yelled the Dutchman, and the Rodent began crying.

"What's going on here?" I said to the Major, who seemed to be the only one who had retained his composure.

"After you evaded us," he said, "we got to discussing matters, when suddenly it dawned upon me that all of British East has extradition treaties with its neighboring nations. So we sent Le Rongeur to check with the police, and found that they had no record of a Captain Peter Clarke."

"I don't understand," I said with a sinking feeling in the pit of my stomach.

"You damned imbecile!" shrieked the Rodent, wiping the tears from his face. "You turned the money over to Erich Von Horst!"

I was struck dumb for a minute. Then I raced out the door and ran for the waterfront with the Major, the Rodent, and the Dutchman close on my heels. When we arrived the Dutchman pointed out the pier where the ship was docked, and we got there just in time to see it putting out to sea.

Von Horst, still dressed in his British police uniform, was standing on the deck, and as his eyes fell upon us a broad smile spread over his face. Then he bowed deeply, straightened up, and gave us a snappy German military salute just before the fog obscured him and the boat (and the Tabernacle of Saint Luke) from my vision.

I left my companions weeping and cursing on the pier, silently promised the Lord never to offer my pearls to swine again, gathered up my few worldly possessions, and left quietly so as not to disturb the desk clerk. Then, pausing only long enough to refresh my spirit at Maurice's, I left the sinful city of Dar-es-Salaam behind me and set forth once again to do the Good Lord's bidding.

3. THE VAMPIRE

How I met Herbie Miller and made eighteen thousand dollars in twenty-seven days came about like this:

Shortly after I took my leave of Dar-es-Salaam I did a little computing and figured out that fifty British pounds, which was all I had in my pocket, wasn't quite enough to start building my tabernacle. So I went out into the wilderness (of which there was an awful lot back in those days) and had a little conference with my Silent Partner, Who advised me that if I was to properly carry on His work I'd need considerably more in the way of a grubstake. It was about this time that Karamojo Bell and Deaf Banks and Pondoro Taylor and John Alfred Jordan were making big names and even bigger fortunes for themselves by the killing of elephants, and I figured that with God to guide my bullets, knocking off a few tons of ivory shouldn't be so very difficult.

Of course, I did have a couple of minor problems. For one thing, I didn't know the first thing about tracking or killing elephants, and in fact had never even held a rifle in my hands. For another, elephant licenses were very expensive, though since the Tabernacle of Saint Luke was to be a nonprofit enterprise I felt certain that the purchasing of licenses didn't really apply to me. Just the same, Kenya and Tanganyika were pretty well patrolled by game wardens and various other gendarmes who might view the license situation more narrowly, which meant that I would have to go to the Interior to find my fortune. I had heard tell of huge herds of elephants in the Lado Enclave, a large and savage area just west of Uganda. This wasn't officially in Africa's dark Interior, but it was Interior enough for me, since I didn't know where to begin looking for it.

I took the East African Railway to the railhead in Uganda, a long and arduous trip which left me barely enough money to buy an old military rifle. I spent my last couple of pounds buying bullets, and then asked the local constabulary to direct me to the Enclave. He waved his hand in a northerly direction which covered approximately three-quarters of Uganda, and so, armed only with my rifle and a copy of the Good Book, I began my career as an ivory hunter.

I had walked about fifteen miles when night fell, and I spent a chilly few hours communing with God and Nature out in the African bush. I awoke stiff and hungry, especially hungry, and decided to hone my aim while shooting down a little something for breakfast.

I began walking through the grasslands and came upon an old waterbuck grazing alone. Seventeen shots later he was still grazing, and I began to realize that there was more to hunting than I had been led to believe. After my first two shots thudded home into a tree some fifty feet from him, he didn't even bother to run away, but just stared at me for a moment and then went back to his grazing.

I kept walking north for the better part of a week, living on a diet of fruits and berries, and wondering how I was going to kill an entire herd of elephants unless they stood in a nice long nose-to-tail line so that my bullets were bound to hit *something*. The vegetation was getting pretty lush, which meant that the ticks and flies and spiders and mosquitoes were out in force. Then one afternoon I saw a native village in the distance, and remembering my experience with Kitunga's friends and relations, I decided to give it a wide berth. As I was doing so I came to an undersized and undernourished white man staked out in the sun.

"Good day to you, brother," I said, walking up to him.

"Good afternoon, friend," he replied, turning his head to get a better look at me.

"Lovely day," I said, wondering what to say or do next.

"Think it may rain, though," he said.

I looked up at the sky. "Not enough clouds. The rainy season is just about over. By the way, brother, are you trussed up on the ground for any particular reason?"

"None that I happen to agree with, friend," he said. "It was done to me by a vile and barbarous tribe called the Ankole. I wonder if you, being a God-fearing Christian and a white man to boot, would mind cutting me loose of these here stakes?"

"Well, brother," I said, "it does seem the Christian thing to do. On the other hand, I passed an Ankole village not too far from here, and they might not understand a gesture of Christian charity." I sat down beside him to mull it over in my mind. "What did you do that set them against you?"

"They objected to some of my personal tastes and habits," he said, blinking his eyes to get some of the sweat out.

"You're not some kind of moral degenerate, are you?" I said, my good pious blood starting to boil about the edges.

"Perish the thought, neighbor!" he said vigorously. "It was a simple misunderstanding. Now won't you be a gentleman and cut a fellow white man free?"

"I've got to weigh the question carefully," I said, shooting a glance in the direction of the village to see if any of them were approaching us.

"Well, in the meantime," he said, his skin kind of twitching, "you wouldn't have any insect repellent with you, would you, friend?"

"Sorry," I said. "You must be right uncomfortable."

"Well, it's getting kind of warm, what with the sun beating down on me and insects crawling all over me," he admitted. "How about some gin? Being staked out like this is mighty dry work." A tsetse fly landed on his face and began crawling up his nose.

"What's your name, brother?" I asked, shooing the fly away.

"Miller," he said. "Herbie Miller, from Amarillo, Texas."

"Well, I'm pleased to make your acquaintance, Brother Miller," I said, extending my hand and then quickly withdrawing it when I realized that he was in no position to respond in kind. "And I'm the Honorable Doctor Lucifer Jones, pastor of the Tabernacle of Saint Luke."

"Pleased to meet you," said Herbie. "I'd get up, but . . ."

"I quite understand, Brother Miller. What's a fellow like you doing out here in the wilderness anyway?"

"I was fighting as a mercenary for the British against the Germans in Tanganyika during the Great War, but they threw me out, and I've been wandering around Africa ever since."

"Why did they throw you out?" I asked.

"Personality conflict," he said.

"With the whole British army?"

"I'd like to go into the matter in greater detail," said Herbie, "but there's a poisonous scorpion crawling up my leg, and I fear that my story may come to an abrupt and painful end if you don't do something about him, Doctor Jones, sir."

I flicked the scorpion away and stomped on it. Then the Good Lord took a hand in the proceedings and hit me with another of His revelations.

"When you were in the army, did you ever have occasion to fire a rifle?" I asked.

"I most certainly did," said Herbie. "You know, I'd even settle for a little taste of vodka."

"How good a shot were you?"

"A crackerjack shot, sir," said Herbie. "But you needn't worry, Doctor Jones. I'd never turn on the man who set me free, and besides, I don't have any weapons with me."

"You ever shoot an elephant?" I asked.

"On occasion," he said. Then his face tensed up. "Don't tell me there's an elephant about to charge us!"

"Wouldn't think of it," I said, pulling out a jackknife and cutting his bonds.

"Thank you, Doctor Jones," he said, rising to his feet and rubbing some circulation back into his extremities.

I threw a friendly arm around his shoulders. "Think nothing of it, Brother Miller. After all, what are partners for?"

"Partners?" he said.

I nodded.

We left the area right quick, not wishing to run into any Ankole tribesmen who might not understand the fact that I couldn't leave a fellow white man to the mercies of the elements, and headed on up to the outpost of Arua, just a handful of miles from the Uganda-Congo border.

"How much money do you have?" I asked Herbie.

"Maybe five pounds," he said, pulling out some faded, miscolored bills and a handful of coins.

"Give it to me," I said, "and wait for me about a mile west of town."

"That's all the money I have in the world," he protested. "How do I know you'll come back?"

I tossed the rifle to him. "Keep this as security."

He began walking to the west, and I entered the outpost and sought out the local bar. I waited for the better part of an hour, until a pair of men dressed in British military uniforms came in. Inside of five minutes everyone else had left and I walked up to the bar, announcing in a loud voice that I'd like to buy a drink for everyone in the house. They looked around, figured out that I meant them, and invited me to join them at their table.

"Pleased to meet you, brothers," I said. "I'm the Honorable Right Reverend Doctor Jones, preaching my way across this savage continent."

"Pleased to make your acquaintance," said the older of the two men. "I'm Captain Michael Holmes, and this is Lieutenant Richard Thorpe. Where are you heading for?"

"Wherever I can bring peace and contentment to my fellow man," I said devoutly. "I'll go anyplace where the spirit of these godless savages needs uplifting."

"That's highly commendable," said Lieutenant Thorpe. "I wish there were more people like you, Padre."

"Why, thank you kindly, Brother Thorpe," I said, signaling the bartender to bring the bottle. "Have another drink."

We got to talking for a while then, and drinking pretty hard, and before long we were all loosened up and pretty good friends.

"I just think it's wonderful," said Captain Holmes after a long silence.

"What is?" I asked.

"A man of God going fearlessly through the bush, bringing the Word and the Spirit to the savages."

"There's no resisting the call once it comes to rest on you, brother," I said modestly. "However, I'd be lying if I didn't tell you that I'm far from fearless."

"Certainly you are," objected Captain Holmes. "How could you be a coward, rubbing shoulders with cannibals and pygmies and the like?"

"I'll tell you, Brother Holmes," I said. "Not all of us are afraid of the same things. Now, as for me, I know that all men are God's children, so I don't have no fear when I walk into a native village. But that don't mean I ain't afraid of other things."

"Such as?"

"Such as elephants, Brother Holmes," I said with a shudder. "Creatures of Satan they are, with them incredible proboscises and little red eyes, and able to crush the life out of a man so easy-like." I downed another drink emphatically.

"Nothing to worry about, Padre," said Thorpe. "There's no elephants within twenty miles of here."

"A comfort," I said. "A definite comfort. But my call has been made clear to me, brothers. I got to go through some place called the Conclave or something like that, and I'm told that it's absolutely rife with bloodthirsty pachyderms."

"You mean the Lado Enclave?" asked Holmes.

"The very spot!" I said. "The very spot indeed. I don't suppose I could, as one good Christian to another, ask one of you gentlemen to escort me safely through there so's I don't fall prey to some elephant's dark and bloodthirsty desires?"

"I'm afraid not, Padre," said Thorpe. "We're on duty here. But elephants are a pretty peaceful lot, by and large. If you see any, just give them a wide berth."

"Do one of you gentlemen have a map of the area?" I asked, pouring them each another drink.

Holmes pulled a map out of his vest pocket and unfolded it. "Here you are, Reverend Jones," he said.

I found the Lado Enclave right quick, and estimated it to be a day-and-a-half march to the north and west. Then I picked a pencil out of my pocket and handed it to Thorpe.

"I wonder, Brother Thorpe," I said, "if you could mark the areas of the Enclave I'll most want to avoid?"

"You mean places with . . ."

I nodded and gulped in terror. "Right. With elephants."

He looked at the map, then drew seven or eight circles at various parts of the Enclave. "Okay, Reverend Jones," he said at last. "These represent the greatest concentrations of the herds. If you just walk around these areas you should be okay. You may run into a stray elephant now and then, but you'll avoid most of them."

"I don't know how to thank you, brothers," I said, folding up the map and sticking it inside my shirt. "You can't begin to know what a service you've done for the Lord this day."

"Always happy to help a man of the cloth," said Thorpe. "As for thanking us, it's not necessary—though if you run across any ivory poachers, you might report them to us on your next swing through here."

"I certainly will," I said, "though I can't understand why anyone would kill elephants."

"I would have thought you'd approve," said Holmes.

"For vengeance, yes," I said. "But for profit? That's breaking the Second and Ninth Commandments."

I took my leave of them then, and wandered off to meet Herbie.

"What have you been doing?" he demanded when I got there.

"Securing our fortune," I said, throwing the map down in front of him. "I supply the brainpower, you supply the marksmanship, and we split the take."

"Fifty-fifty?" he asked.

"One-third, one-third, one-third," I corrected him.

"Come again?" said Herbie.

"One-third for you, one-third for me, and one-third for the Lord."

He kept insisting that this was really a two-to-one split for me, so after some further haggling we finally decided on fifty-five percent of the first ten thousand pounds for me, forty-five percent for Herbie, and the Lord had an option on the next three thousand pounds.

We decided that we'd better be up and on the trail bright and early the next morning, so we turned in almost immediately. During the middle of the night I felt a sharp pain in the side of my neck, and, figuring it was some small lizard or beetle, I tried to flick it off with my hand, and wound up poking Herbie in the eye.

"Goddamnit!" he screamed, rubbing his eye vigorously. "What did you want to go and do that for, Lucifer?"

"Why don't you tell me just what you were doing bending over my neck?" I snapped.

"It's personal," moaned Herbie, still holding his hand over his eye.

"It's more than personal," I said. "It's perverted! Kissing a man's neck when he's sleeping!"

"I wasn't kissing you, Lucifer," he whined. "Honest I wasn't."

"Just see that it don't happen again," I said, and lay back down on my blanket.

And not ten minutes later I felt this pain in my neck again.

"Herbie!" I yelled, and he must have jumped five feet into the air. "What the hell is going on?"

"Well, Lucifer," he sighed, "you might as well know the truth."

"That you're some kind of moral degenerate?"

"No."

"Then what?"

"I'm a vampire," he said.

"You mean like goes around sucking blood and such?" I said.

He nodded sadly. "I wish I wasn't. I mean, you have no idea the strain it puts me under, but I am and that's all there is to it."

"How long have you been a vampire?"

"Oh, about ten years now. Maybe eleven. You know, Lucifer, I don't think there's any group anywhere in the world that's more misunderstood than us vampires. I mean, I hope you don't think I *like* nabbing people in the neck and drinking their blood." He shuddered. "It's disgusting!"

"Then why do you do it?"

"I'm compelled to, just like you're compelled to drink water," he answered. "It's not a matter of choice."

"But I've seen you in the sunlight," I said. "I thought vampires couldn't do that."

"European vampires can't," said Herbie. "It's like a whole different union."

"I've seen you eat meat," I said.

"I've seen you eat meat, too," he shot back. "Doesn't stop you from needing water, does it?"

"Is this why you were kicked out of the army?" I asked.

He nodded.

"And why the Ankole had you staked out?"

"Yes," he said. "Believe me, Lucifer, I'm a better person for being able to talk about it. I'm not like this all the time, really I'm not. Most of the time I'm just as normal as you are. It's just that sometimes I . . . well, I get this *craving*."

"Do you have it now?" I asked.

He stared long and hard at my neck. "No," he said with a relieved sigh. "I think it's gone now." He paused for a moment, then nodded vigorously. "Yes, I'm sure it's gone."

"Good," I said, walking over and tying him to a tree. "I'll let you loose in the morning." I went back to my blanket and lay down. "I think I'll probably be tying you up every night. Nothing personal, you understand."

"I understand. You've no idea how comforting it is to be able to talk about this with someone," he said, just as I was drifting off to sleep. "You know, some missionaries have set up a hospital over in

Masindi, and they probably have a fair supply of blood there. I don't suppose we could—"

"No, we couldn't!" I said, and fell asleep.

We spent the next day foot-slogging, and by mid-morning of the second day we had reached the outskirts of the Lado Enclave. We made camp early and fell to studying Captain Michael Holmes' map, trying to figure out the quickest way to get to the nearest of the herds. Finally we bedded down, and were up about an hour before sunrise.

We began finding piles of fresh elephant dung about noon, and within about two hours had snuck to within a quarter mile of a herd of maybe two hundred of the beasts. Herbie lay down on his belly, tested the wind with a handful of dry dirt, and began inching forward. I looked at him for a minute, then did the same.

Since I was bigger than Herbie I began getting a little ahead of him, and I stopped when we were about eighty yards away from a huge bull with enormous tusks. Then, just as I was about to suggest that we were close enough for a shot, Herbie sank his teeth into the side of my neck.

I let out a yell, and all hell broke loose. The elephants stood in a circle, trunks extended, trying to figure out where the noise had come from, and then three or four of them started running straight at us.

I jumped up, more mad at Herbie than scared of the elephants, and pointed down at the little vampire, who was nibbling on my Achilles tendon.

"He's the one!" I screamed at the oncoming elephants. "Just run right by me and flatten that little bloodsucker!"

The elephants wheeled around like quarter horses and raced off in the other direction the second they saw and heard me, and a moment later there wasn't an animal to be seen anywhere, except for the one who was slowly getting up next to me.

"I don't know what happened, Lucifer," he said. "I've never done that in the daytime before."

"You damned fool!" I screamed. "You could have gotten us both killed!"

He just hung his head and looked so sad that all the anger evaporated right out of me.

"All right," I said, patting him on the shoulder. "Just try to give me a little warning next time we're sneaking up on a herd of elephants, okay?"

Well, the next time didn't come for almost a week, during which time Herbie tried marching to his different drummer more and more often, especially if I would nick myself while shaving. But finally one morning we found about a dozen young males and one real old one with huge tusks lolling in a small wooded glen.

This time I made sure Herbie went ahead of me, and when he got within about forty yards of them he cut loose with a couple of shots and dropped the old tusker. I ran up to look at the corpse, and discovered that Herbie was nowhere to be seen.

"Herbie!" I called.

"Up here, Lucifer," he replied, and I looked up and found him perched in a tree about twenty-five feet above the ground.

"What are you doing up there?" I said.

"There's always a chance that one of the others will come back," he said, "and you've got all the rest of the bullets."

"That shows a lot of foresight," I said.

"Thank you, Lucifer."

"What am *I* supposed to do if one of them comes back?"

He paused thoughtfully, then asked, "How good are you at climbing trees?"

"Not very," I said.

"Oh," he said. "Well, do you know any real fast prayers?"

"Knock off the comedy and come down here," I said.

"That wasn't a rhetorical question, Lucifer," he said. "There's an elephant about fifty feet behind you, and he looks very unhappy."

Which was how I found out that I could climb trees after all.

We stayed on our branches for an hour or two after the elephant had left, then climbed cautiously down and examined our ivory.

"Looks like about one hundred and thirty pounds a tusk," I said.

"At least," said Herbie. Then, "Lucifer, I've got a question."

"What is it, Herbie?"

"How are we going to get the tusks off the elephant?"

It was a right smart question at that. We spent the better part of the afternoon hunting up long sharp stones, and all of the next day chopping away at the tusks. Herbie got thirsty in his unique way toward late morning, and I damned near flattened his head with my stone, after which he was well behaved for the rest of the day. By nightfall we had managed to chop off the tusks, and not a moment too soon, since our elephant wasn't turning into any nosegay and the vultures were getting dangerously low in the sky.

"Now what?" asked Herbie.

"Now we carry them back to camp," I said.

"I don't know about you, Lucifer," said Herbie, "but I don't think I can lift my tusk."

"Of course you can," I said.

"I only weigh about a hundred and ten pounds," said Herbie.

"Try dragging it," I said.

So he tried. He got it about forty feet away from the carcass and collapsed.

"Okay," I said. "I'll tell you what we'll do. Grab the front end of my tusk, I'll take the rear end, and we'll cart it to camp like that and then come back for the other one."

He agreed, and we started off through the bush. It was two hours later when we staggered into camp, and we decided not to go back for the other tusk until the next morning. Poor Herbie was so exhausted that he didn't even try to nab me in the neck that night before I tied him up, and I literally had to kick him awake the next morning. Then, stiff and sore and aching in every muscle, we set out for our other tusk.

We never did find it. All them bushes and trees and rivers and trails got to looking alike, and after about seven or eight hours we had to admit we were as lost as two people were ever likely to get.

We wandered for another day or two and couldn't even find our original camp. Finally, on our third day of searching, we came to a Wanderobo village, where we were given a red-carpet treatment and feted like visiting ambassadors.

The chief was a nice old boy called Nmumba, and he had picked up a smattering of English from various hunters and traders over the years. He sat us by his campfire, surrounded us with his naked daughters, and served us a native brew that was even more potent than Kitunga's. Every now and then he'd make a joke. The way we knew this was he'd goose one of his daughters and she'd shriek like all get-out, and this was our signal to laugh.

I was wondering what to do with Herbie, because it was getting near bedtime, and it somehow didn't seem proper to truss him up while we were in Nmumba's village. I mentioned this to him, and he looked downright serious as he answered me.

"I really think you'd better tie me up tonight, Lucifer," he said. "I've been getting the craving real bad. I suppose it's all them naked necks."

"If you say so," I said. "Also, I have a feeling that he'd be something less than a gentleman if he didn't offer us a couple of his daughters for the night."

"I'll never be able to make it!" said Herbie. "I'm getting thirsty just thinking about them!"

I made our excuses and took Herbie off to a hut where I tied him up to one of the support poles.

"If he offers us his daughters, I'll accept both of them just as a matter of good manners," I said as I was securing the knots. "But don't you worry none, Brother Herbie: It's my Christian duty to keep them away from you."

Which it was, and which I did.

When I got up in the morning Nmumba decided to show me around the village, being careful to explain that it was only a temporary dwelling place since the Wanderobo are basically nomads, but that it was ours as long as his tribe remained there. Finally we walked over to a huge hut that had to be holding a good ten tons of ivory.

"That's a mighty impressive-looking collection, Brother Nmumba," I said, figuring out its worth down to the nearest shilling.

He looked pleased as punch. "The Wanderobo are mighty hunters," he said.

"No question about that," I replied. "Did you kill them all with spears?"

"Yes," said Nmumba proudly.

"So tell me, Brother Nmumba," I said, "if the hunting is so good here, why are you moving your people out of the Enclave?"

"Need new *juju* man."

"You mean a witch doctor?"

He nodded. "Our *juju* man died four moons ago, and we fear for our children's health."

"They all looked pretty healthy to me," I said.

"Our last *juju* man made strong *juju*," said Nmumba. "But soon it will wear off, and we must find another before my people sicken and die."

"It's nothing catching, is it?" I asked, backing off a bit just out of good manners.

"No. It is . . . I have not words for it."

Well, we got to using sign language, and just the merest bit of Swahili I had picked up, and it turned out that this particular *juju* was a form of preventative medicine. I knew they didn't have no vaccinations out in the wilderness, so I questioned him about the nature of it.

"Cut veins," said Nmumba.

"I'm not sure I follow you, Brother Nmumba," I said.

"Cut like so," he said, pointing to a recently healed knife scar just between his earlobe and his jawbone. "Bad blood goes out. Devils go out."

"You mean the old *juju* man *bled* you?"

He nodded. "Very strong medicine."

It wasn't the first time I'd heard of bleeding as a disease preventive. In fact, it had been all the rage in the courts of Europe for centuries. But it was kind of surprising to find it being practiced out here in the bush.

And then I realized that it was more than surprising—it was Providential.

"Brother Nmumba," I said, "I think this may be your lucky day. My friend is a *juju* man, one of the greatest in all Africa."

"Too small," said Nmumba doubtfully.

"Big things come in small packages, Brother Nmumba," I said. "Not only can Brother Herbie bleed your people, but he will take all the devils into his own body so they can never harm you again."

"Truly?" said Nmumba.

"Do I look like the kind of man who would lie to you?" I said. "Brother Nmumba, you cut me to the quick!"

Nmumba lowered his head in thought for a moment. "Would he agree to be our *juju* man?"

"Nothing would please him more," I said truthfully.

"Good!" said Nmumba. "Then it is settled, and the Wanderobo can remain here for many moons."

"Well, there is one little problem," I said.

"Oh?"

"It would mean that my own people would be without a *juju* man, and in exchange for this they would probably want some compensation. Not for myself, you understand; I'm happy just to be able to do my good friend Nmumba a favor. But they will probably have to go out and hire another *juju* man."

He didn't understand many of the words, but the message came across loud and clear. We sat down for some hard bargaining, and half an hour later I had traded Herbie Miller to the Wanderobo for twelve thousand pounds of ivory and porters to carry it down to Mombasa for me.

Which is how I made my first fortune, and how Herbie Miller became the happiest witch doctor on the entire Dark Continent.

4. SLAVE TRADING

It was with a certain feeling of quiet pride and accomplishment that I led my seventy porters eastward toward civilization, carrying a modest fortune of ivory on their broad, sweat-streaked backs. We marched for about three days, and headed north toward the Sudan just to make sure that we didn't bother any game wardens or British officers who might have been in the area, which is how I lost my fortune before I had a chance to build my tabernacle.

One night we were lying down by the campfire, totally exhausted—them from toting all that ivory, and me from converting it into dollars inside my head—when a bunch of shots rang out and pretty soon we were surrounded by a dozen Arabs in full desert regalia. Now, I know that on the surface it seems kind of hard to envision twelve men surrounding seventy-one, but it's a lot easier than you might think when the twelve men have rifles and the seventy-one don't.

Anyway, they motioned me to step aside, and herded the porters into a tight little circle, making them kneel down and raise their hands above their heads, a gesture I was not unacquainted with, but had previously seen only on Sunday mornings and in games of chance involving little white cubes with spots painted on them.

"Not a bad haul," said a familiar voice. "And ivory, too! Not bad at all, my friends."

Then a fat man in a soiled white suit stepped out of the shadows and nodded to me.

"Dutchman!" I exclaimed.

"Doctor Jones," he replied with a smile. "What a pleasant surprise to see you once again, my good friend."

"What the hell is going on here?" I demanded.

"I am afraid that *you* are responsible for my presence here, my dear Doctor Jones," smiled the Dutchman, pulling out a handkerchief and wiping the sweat from his pudgy face.

"Me?"

"Indeed. You see, when Herr Von Horst made off with a certain shipment of, shall we say, perishable goods, purchasing them with funds that you freely gave to him, I found that I had to expand my primary business to make up for the income you had cost me. Regrettable, to be sure, but fitting in a way, would you not agree?"

"I most certainly would not!" I snapped. "That ivory and them porters are mine! Though, of course, if you want to rent them from me once they deliver the tusks, I'm sure we can do a little business."

"Oh, no, my friend," laughed the Dutchman. "I'm doing my business right now. You wouldn't happen to know your wrist and ankle sizes, would you?"

"Surely you're not thinking about putting shackles and chains on a fellow white man, Brother Dutchman?" I said in horror.

"What guarantee have I that you won't try to run away before we reach our destination?" he asked, putting a pudgy hand to his chin and eyeing me warily.

"You've got my word as a Christian gentleman and a man of honor," I replied.

"Get the chains!" he called to one of his Arabs.

"Brother Dutchman!" I cried. "It's inhuman to chain me like I was some black heathen on the way to market. Surely we can work out some accommodation that would be mutually acceptable."

"Oh, it's just for a little while, Doctor Jones," he said. "Once we get into the desert, I'll be happy to release you."

"You will?"

"Certainly. After all, I'll have the only water for hundreds of miles in any direction."

And so I was chained, hand and foot and neck, to my seventy porters. Out of deference to my race and my position, the Dutchman chained me first in line, which struck me as only just and fitting, until I figured out that the first man in line was also the first to step on snakes and scorpions and other foul denizens of the desert. And, of course, anytime one of the porters tripped or even slowed down, I usually found out about it in an exceptionally painful and undignified way.

Then there was the matter of the ivory. The Dutchman didn't want to leave it behind, but it was kind of hard for the porters to carry, shackled up as they were, so we had to stop every half hour or so for them to shift the weight.

Finally, on the second evening of my captivity, after our neck chains were unhooked for the night, I moseyed over to where the Dutchman was sitting alone by his fire.

"Mind if I join you?" I asked, sitting down next to him as gracefully as my chains would allow.

"As a matter of fact, I do," he replied, taking a swig from a half-empty flask of something that sure didn't smell much like water. "After all, how will it look to the hired help? I don't even let *them* share my fire or my liquid refreshments."

He gestured to the twelve rifle-toting Arabs, who were eyeing me with open hostility.

"Besides," he continued, "I try never to mix business with pleasure. If we got to talking and drinking and swapping lies, I'd feel absolutely miserable about what I'm going to be doing to you in a week."

"Oh?" I said.

"Yes, Doctor Jones. It would fair break my heart. On the whole, I think it would be best if you were to quickly take leave of me and return to your porters."

"Well, actually I didn't come over here to swap lies with you, Brother Dutchman," I said.

"Well, if we're speaking business, that's a whole different matter," said the Dutchman, suddenly alert. He offered the flask to me. "Have a drink, Doctor Jones."

"Don't mind if I do," I said, taking a long sip and then another. "How much ivory do you suppose I've got here with me, Brother Dutchman?"

"None," he replied with a smile. "But if I understand the thrust of your question, I've got about eighteen thousand dollars' worth."

"There's a lot more where that came from," I said softly, which was technically true, since it had originally come from elephants, and as far as I knew there wasn't any current and severe shortage of them.

"You're suggesting that if I release you you'll lead me to all this ivory?" asked the Dutchman with a sly grin.

I nodded, returning his grin.

"Well, I do wish I could accommodate you, Doctor Jones," he said, still smiling, "but the porters can hardly carry what we've got now. Besides, ivory is very difficult to sell in Egypt, whereas . . . But I think you get the point."

"Say no more, Brother Dutchman," I said confidently. "If it's more black heathen you want, I can round 'em up and have 'em here in no time."

"You still don't seem to understand," said the Dutch man. "Everyone sells natives. Natives are a drug on the market. It is you, Doctor Jones, who constitutes the *piece de resistance* of my current consignment."

"Me?" I repeated.

"You," he said, nodding sadly. "And because I have nothing against you personally, other than the fact that you cost me a modest fortune back in Dar-es-Salaam, and are a scoundrel and liar to boot, I must confess to you that it grieves me more deeply than you can imagine to have to sell you to Ali ben Ishak, no matter how much he pays me."

"Ali ben Ishak?"

He nodded again.

"Nasty fellow, is he?" I asked as a small knot formed in my belly and began to grow.

"Under other circumstances I wouldn't wish your fate on my worst enemy," said the Dutchman gravely.

"Tell me about him," I said.

"Please, my friend," said the Dutchman, holding up a hand for silence. "I wish to speak no further on the subject. It would only depress me."

"If it upsets you all that much, Dutchman," I suggested, "perhaps it might be better not to sell me to this Ishak person after all."

"My dear fellow," he said severely, "this is *business*. I'll just have to learn to live with the guilt."

That being settled, he had another swallow from his flask and ambled off to his tent. His Arabs shooed me away from the fire, and I rejoined my porters, thinking that maybe they weren't such unfortunate souls after all, at least compared to some people I could name, like me for instance.

The next three days passed pretty uneventfully, unless you think trudging across a desert with your hands and feet chained together qualifies as an event. At that point, which was five days into our little sojourn, the Dutchman had one of his Arabs unshackle me after first explaining that we were at least a four-day march from water of any kind.

Now, I could find a lot of fault with the Dutchman's ethics and morals and appearance and even his personal hygiene, but I'd never noticed much wrong with his business sense, so when he told me that I took him at his word and made no attempt to sneak off from the caravan. Besides, he still had my ivory, and without it the Tabernacle of Saint Luke wasn't likely to get itself built in the real near future.

Every day I'd ask the Dutchman about this Ali ben Ishak character, and every day he'd tell me that he was too fond of me to discuss the matter. The only thing he'd say was that Ali ben Ishak was one of the five wealthiest Arabs in the world, and that he (the Dutchman) felt just terrible about this whole situation. I must confess that the more I tried to talk about it, the more he wasn't the only one who felt terrible. Finally I decided to put the entire thing in the hands of the Lord, after explaining the problem to Him and making certain recommendations of my own. Thereafter I spoke no more about it, and concentrated mostly on not dying of heat stroke, a considerable task in its own right.

It was a week to the day since we'd been captured that I looked ahead of me and saw a huge cloud of sand out near the horizon. It came closer, and finally I could make out a batch of Arab sheikhs and warriors mounted on horseback and camels, all wearing colorful robes and headgear and sporting expensive-looking rifles. The Dutchman signaled us to stop and then had us walk in a circle, just like the old-time pioneers did whenever Indians drew near. Then he had his dozen men brandish their weapons and position themselves around our close-knit little group.

The leader of the mounted Arabs signaled his own men to stop about twenty yards away. Then he rode his horse slowly toward me and the Wanderobo, circled us twice, and turned to the Dutchman.

"Slaves?" he asked, cocking an eyebrow.

"Friends and relations," said the Dutchman hastily.

"In chains?" asked the old sheikh.

"I don't get along with them very well," answered the Dutchman.

"Where are you going?" asked the sheikh.

"Nairobi," said the Dutchman.

"You're heading in the wrong direction," said the sheikh.

"We thought we'd get a little exercise along the way," said the Dutchman.

"And who are you?" asked the Arab.

"Colonel T. E. Lawrence," replied the Dutchman. "But my friends call me El Aurens."

Suddenly the old sheikh's attitude changed, and he became positively servile. After offering Allah's blessings on the Dutchman and his friends and relations, he rejoined his men and beat a hasty path around us.

"That was close!" sighed the Dutchman, wiping some sweat from his forehead.

"How did you know they'd leave you alone if you told them you were Lawrence of Arabia?" I asked.

"Trial and error. One batch almost tore me apart when I told them I was Chinese Gordon. I guess they don't view the fall of Khartoum quite the same way you and I do. Anyway, after a number of confrontations, I found that Lawrence's name worked best."

"And what will happen if the real Lawrence ever shows up?" I asked.

"I imagine they'll think he's Chinese Gordon and tear him to pieces," replied the Dutchman with a chuckle.

He walked over to me and attached me to the porters again. "I hate to do this to you, my friend," he grated as he was attaching the chains, "but we reach Cairo in two more days and I wouldn't want you to do anything unwise."

I promptly asked the Lord to strike him down and set me free, but evidently my Silent Partner was otherwise occupied at the time, for I spent the next two days in chains, walking north to Cairo.

It was dark when we got to the outskirts of the city. We made camp about three miles from one of the poorer sections, of which there were an awful lot, lit a campfire, and allowed the Arabs to ply us with a number of bottles of native beer. When I remarked upon the Dutchman's generosity, he replied that while it was undoubtedly true that he was the very soul of generosity, it would also serve to make us look a little fatter on the auction block the next morning.

"And now, Doctor Jones," he added with a strange glint in his eye, "I think it is time for my men to unshackle you and bring you over here for a bath."

They did so, and I must confess that the Dutchman prepared the bath of my life for me. It was sweet-smelling and filled with all kinds of soaps and oils. Then, after I dried myself off, the Dutchman himself gave me a haircut and a shave, after which two of the Arabs gave me a rubdown and poured more oils onto me.

When all this was done the Dutchman handed me back my clothes, which had been washed while all this other preparation was going on. I got into them, and then he stood back, hands on hips, and just kind of stared at me.

"Oh, yes," he said at last. "Eighty thousand Maria Theresa dollars, at the very least."

Well, this made absolutely no sense to me, because as far as I could see the whole damned lot of us *plus* the ivory wasn't going to bring anything near eighty thousand dollars. And while Ali ben Ishak may very well have been one of the richest men in the world, rich folk didn't get that way by over-tipping, or remembering the cook's birthday, or bidding eighty thousand dollars for a slave in a bear market.

Still, if it made the Dutchman happy to think otherwise, it was no skin off my back—and keeping my skin on my back had suddenly become pretty imperative to me.

Pretty soon the Dutchman and the Arabs began drinking the leftover beer, and since I was still unchained I kind of helped them a bit. It must have been a lot stronger than I thought, because in about half an hour only the Dutchman was still awake, and he and I got to talking about old times and sipping generously from his flask, and within another ten minutes or so he was out cold.

I gave serious consideration to trying to free the porters, but I didn't want to chance waking up any of the Arabs while searching for the keys to their chains, and besides, *some*one had to stick around to carry all that ivory back to Mombasa, so I just gave them a brief but friendly smile and raced off toward the city.

Being in my usual marvelous condition, and a fine figure of a man as well, it took me only a couple of hours to negotiate the intervening three miles, and I arrived in Cairo hardly panting at all. I must have come in the back way or something, because while there were a lot of huge palaces at the far end of town, I was in an area of twisting streets and little white shacks. I asked two or three locals for directions but they kept speaking some foreign tongue so I just kept on walking past the bazaars and the ramshackle housing and such until I suddenly found myself on what seemed to be a main road.

I hopped on the back of a slow-moving double-decker bus, rode about a mile, and slipped off without distracting the conductor from his appointed duties. Finally I saw a white man in a white suit just like the Dutchman's, only not so soiled, and wearing a straw hat, and I walked up to him.

"Good evening, brother," I said.

"No handouts," he grunted, and kept walking.

"Now, brother," I said, falling into step beside him, "do I look like a man in need of a handout? I happen to be the Right Reverend Doctor Jones, pastor of the Tabernacle of Saint Luke from down south of here."

"Must be a mighty small church," he grated. "There's nothing but sand south of here."

"What direction are we walking?" I said quickly.

"North, you numbskull," he said with some distaste.

"Well, that explains it," I said. "My church is to the east of here. I just got turned around a little."

He stopped, hands on hips, and glared at me. "Just what the hell is it that you want?" he demanded.

"Nothing much, brother," I replied. "I just need some directions."

"Well?" he persisted.

"If you were looking for a slave market in Cairo, just where do you suppose you'd find it?" I asked at last.

"I don't traffic in slaves," he said coldly.

"Neither do I," I assured him quickly. "In fact, it's my intention to buy a batch of them poor lost souls and set them free."

"A noble sentiment," he said, still looking a mite suspicious. "However, I still can't help you. Now, if you'll just stop following me, I'll—"

"Just a minute!" I said, suddenly smitten by another revelation. "Where would I find Ali ben Ishak?"

"What would someone like *you* want with someone like *him*?" he demanded.

"He's my partner," I replied. "The two of us plan to crisscross the countryside buying slaves and setting them adrift on a sea of freedom."

"Not that I believe a word of all this," he said, "but Ali ben Ishak lives in that huge domed building up ahead."

I looked ahead in the direction he indicated, and saw an enormous building, about the size of the White House, at the top of a mild incline. "That one?" I asked, pointing to it.

"No," he answered. "That's just the governmental palace. Ishak lives in the *big* one over toward the left."

I looked again, and saw a gold-spired building that completely dwarfed the government palace. Each of my porters could have had two rooms and a bath and would probably only have taken up the first floor of the guest wing.

"Thank you, brother," I said, heading off toward Ali ben Ishak's abode. "May the Good Lord look after you." It was a sincere blessing, especially since the Lord hadn't done such an all-fired good job of looking after him so far this evening, what with me having removed his wallet while he was pointing out the government palace to me.

I reached Ali ben Ishak's door in about fifteen minutes. I could tell right off that I wasn't going to have to spend a lot of time searching for a doorbell and wondering how to introduce myself, because two huge Egyptians wearing fancy headdresses and baggy pants and not much else withdrew their wicked-looking swords when I tried to enter.

"What is your business here?" asked one of them in a much higher voice than fit his body.

"Oh, nothing special," I said quickly. "I just stopped by to see if your boss would like to make a friendly little contribution to the Tabernacle of Saint Luke."

"The Master supports no charities," said the other, in an equally falsetto voice.

"Who's talking charity?" I said. "The Tabernacle of Saint Luke is perfectly willing to make an equally friendly contribution to Ali ben Ishak. Why don't one of you boys run off and bring your Master down here?"

The two conferred in low whispers for a moment. Then one of them put two fingers into his mouth and let loose with a shrill whistle, and a minute later another half-naked muscleman in baggy pants and a turban showed up. There was some more whispering, a few gestures, a whole lot of staring at me, and then the new arrival told me to follow him.

And let me tell you, that was some house I followed him through. All the draperies were made of spun gold, and more jewels than you could shake a stick at sat in glass cases along the walls of the main gallery, each being guarded by a swarthy-looking Egyptian with a curved sword. We walked through a dining room that would comfortably have sat twelve or thirteen hundred close friends and admirers, circled a tiled pool that was only a little bit smaller than Lake Victoria, and finally we came to a halt in what sure as blazes seemed like a throne room. At any rate, it was a huge room filled with ornate Persian rugs, and there was only one chair in it, a big, luxurious, cushioned thing that sat smackdab in the middle of the floor.

"I will tell the Master that you are here," said my guide, vanishing through a doorway that was pretty much hidden by some hanging tapestries. Since I found myself alone with a few minutes on my hands, I decided to take a look at some of Ali ben Ishak's trinkets and doodads that were sitting on shelves all over the room, and discovered, with some dismay, that they were all carvings and paintings and other renderings of naked white men, with an occasional white boy thrown in for good measure.

Suddenly it occurred to me why the Dutchman was so sure I'd bring all that money, and I lost no time in heading back the way I'd come in, but as I got to the door two more of those damned Egyptian heathens appeared from nowhere and crossed their swords right in my path. I considered stooping down and walking under the blades but thought better of it and went back to the interior of the throne room, looking vainly for a little dirt to rub onto my skin.

Then a silk-and-satin-clad figure, kind of old and skinny but wearing enough jewelry to make him look twenty and handsome in the eyes of most women, entered from behind the tapestries. I smelled him about three seconds before I saw him, and I stopped worrying about all the scents that the Dutchman had rubbed onto me. They were drowned out by his perfume the moment he entered the room.

"Ali ben Ishak?" I said, extending my hand and thanking the Lord that none of the Arabs had thought to give me a manicure.

"Yes," he purred. "And you are Mister . . . ?"

"*Doctor*," I corrected him. "The Right Reverend Doctor Lucifer Jones at your service. In a manner of speaking," I added hastily.

"And to what do I owe the extreme pleasure of this visit, Doctor Jones?" he asked, staring at me through half-lowered lids, which gave him a sort of cockeyed look.

"I believe we have a little business to transact," I said.

"Have we indeed?" he giggled, easing himself onto the chair.

"Ali ben, my friend, I ain't going to mince words with you," I began. "I have a certain commodity to sell that I just know is going to meet with your approval."

"It already has," he said.

"How can it?" I asked. "You don't even know what I'm talking about."

"I understand perfectly," he simpered.

"Don't go understanding me so all-fired fast," I said quickly. "As I was saying, I've brought this particular commodity all the way from the Lado Enclave at enormous personal expense and hardship, knowing that a man of your taste and status would properly appreciate it."

"I'm sure I will," he breathed.

"You can search the whole of Africa and you won't find none better," I said.

"What an absolutely charming notion!" said Ali ben Ishak, closing his eyes and smiling a very strange smile.

"Well, then," I said, "I suppose we'd better get down to talking price. Brother Ali ben, for anyone else I'd charge thirty or thirty-five thousand dollars, but for you the price is a dirt cheap twenty grand."

"That's more than I'm accustomed to paying," he said petulantly.

"You're getting six tons," I pointed out. "That comes to less than two dollars a pound."

"Six tons?" he screamed. "What are you talking about?"

"Ivory," I said. "What are you talking about?"

"Oh, nothing," he muttered, blushing the prettiest shade of pink I ever did see.

"Have we got a deal?" I asked.

Well, we got to haggling and bargaining, and finally I sold him the ivory for sixteen thousand dollars, which was less than I wanted but also sixteen thousand dollars more than I had, so I guess we were both pretty pleased about it.

"You going to be sending your servants out after it?" I asked.

"Immediately," he replied. "And I trust you will remain as my guest until they return with the ivory."

"It'll be my pleasure, Brother Ali ben," I said, since I could see I didn't have much choice in the matter.

He summoned a pair of his major-domos, and I told them exactly where the goods were. "While you fellows are out there," I added, "I've got eighty-three items for tomorrow's slave auction. Would you be good enough to bring them back and clean 'em up a little for me?"

They looked at Ali ben Ishak, who nodded his approval, and then took their leave.

"Nice fellows," I said.

"They used to be," he answered through pursed lips.

"I read about fellows like that in the Good Book," I said. "They were Enochians or something like that, weren't they?"

He didn't answer but just looked kind of wistful, and I could see that he wasn't in a mood to talk to me anymore, so I ambled off, found myself a goose-feather mattress covered with satin sheets and a fur blanket, and plunked myself down for the night.

One of those squeaky-voiced Enochians woke me in the morning, and I didn't even have time to scrounge up a little something to eat before Ali ben Ishak's whole entourage, including me, were out the door and headed toward the slave market.

It was a grungy, grimy little place just west and a bit south of town, but it was crammed to overflowing with sheikhs and sultans and potentates who were all dressed to the nines. When we got there they were auctioning off an East Indian woman who I wouldn't have minded bidding on myself, and I followed Ali ben Ishak to a row of chairs that seemed to have been set aside especially for him and his retainers.

Next the twelve bleary-eyed Arabs came on as a single unit, and I spent a goodly amount of time rummaging on the floor looking for diamonds and other trinkets that my neighbors might have dropped until they were knocked down for ten thousand dollars and led out of sight and earshot.

And then, cursing so loud we could hear him while he was still outside the building, the Dutchman was dragged up onto the auction block.

"Lot Number 27," announced the auctioneer. He tried to show the Dutchman's teeth to the crowd and almost got his finger bitten off for his trouble.

"There he is!" screamed the Dutchman, catching sight of me. "There's the son of a pig who's responsible for this!"

I stood up and waved to the crowd, who cheered raucously and threw a few coins in my direction.

"You don't understand!" bellowed the Dutchman. "*He's* supposed to be up here being sold! *I'm* supposed to be down there!"

"The man's obviously gone off the deep end, Lord protect him," I said somberly. "I ask you, brothers, to compare our appearances. Do I look like a man who's been dragged through the desert to stand on the block? Or, better still, ask my host and good friend Ali ben Ishak."

That quieted everyone down for a while, and the auctioneer went back to telling the crowd how much work the Dutchman would be happy to do in a thirty-hour day. But Ali ben Ishak paid no attention; instead, he just stared long and hard at me.

"Is something troubling you, Brother Ali ben?" I asked at last.

"I'm just wondering how you did it," he purred.

"Did what?"

"Managed to trade places with the Dutchman. I know who he is, of course."

"I don't suppose you'd like to let that little tidbit of knowledge remain our personal secret, would you?" I said.

"If I tell what I know, you will be put on the auction block," he said, more to himself than to me. "And if I were to bid on you . . ." His voice trailed off and he looked thoughtfully at me.

"Brother Ali ben, I know what you're thinking, and while it's immoral and disgusting and unChristian as all get-out, I just can't bring myself to hold it against you, given that I'm doubtless the handsomest young buck you've ever run across. But a lot of these other guys have been looking at me just the way you have, and it's only fair to warn you that if I go on the block I'll probably cost you a million dollars or more. I have it on good authority that the Sultan of Graustark himself has authorized his agents to go that high for me."

"Oh?" he said, knitting his brows.

"Whereas a rum-soaked, foul-mouthed old sex fiend like the Dutchman ought to go for five thousand dollars tops."

"But he's so . . . so . . ." Ali ben Ishak searched for the right word.

"I know," I said. "But dry him out for a month, starve him for a couple more, and buy him a wig, and you'll be surprised at the change in him. I mean, he'll never look as good as me, Lord knows, but you can make yourself one hell of a bargain."

He lowered his head, lost in thought, for about three minutes. When he rejoined the land of the living, the price on the Dutchman was eight hundred dollars and rising by ten-dollar increments. Ali ben Ishak put in a bid of three thousand, and got him before the opposition could muster a rally.

Then they marched out my seventy porters, and while they were showing off each one's teeth in turn, a big one on the end gestured to me to come up to the platform. I did so, and he leaned over and whispered in my ear.

"It is not commonly known that I speak English," he said.

"It ain't even uncommonly known," I replied in surprise. "Why in tarnation didn't you ever speak to me during that whole goddamned long trek through the desert?"

"I never had anything to say," he replied.

"And now you do?" I asked.

"Oh, yes," he said with a grim smile. "And if you do not find a way to free me and my fellow tribesmen, I am going to say it to everyone in this room. I am sure the auctioneer would like to know that since the Dutchman is in no position to make any claims, he can keep one hundred percent of the proceeds he could realize from your sale, rather than merely his commission."

The auctioneer walked over and gave me an inquiring look, which I answered with a sick little grin. Then I returned to my seat.

"The bidding is open!" announced the auctioneer.

"Four thousand for the lot," said one potentate.

"Five," said another.

"Seven," offered a bejeweled rajah.

"Eight thousand," I said, wondering if my remaining eight thousand was enough to start my tabernacle.

"Nine," said the rajah.

"Ten," I said. "And that's all those lazy bastards are worth!"

"Eleven," said the rajah.

"I told you ten was all they were worth!" I shouted. "You got wax in your ears or something? Twelve, and that's my last bid."

"Thirteen," said the rajah.

"Fourteen," I said. "Maybe I can get that much out of them before the law discovers I own 'em."

"The law?" asked one of the potentates.

"They ate their chief," I answered.

The rajah walked up to the platform and looked them over long and hard. "They really ate their chief?"

"Would I lie to you?" I said.

"Fifteen," he said after much hesitation.

"Sixteen," I said. "They're also homosexual rapists."

Ali Ben Ishak jumped to his feet to make a bid, but I stomped on his toe and he sat back down, cursing. The rajah took another long hard look, shook his head, and walked back to his seat.

"Sold, for sixteen thousand dollars," cried the auctioneer.

I looked at my English-speaking porter, who just grinned at me.

"Turn 'em loose and point 'em south," I said. "I changed my mind. They're just too dangerous to keep."

The auctioneer shrugged, and I heard a voice in the back of the room say, "Well, you know those big-shot American millionaires: easy come, easy go."

The auction ended in another hour, and, once again penniless, I took my leave, more than willing to let Ali ben Ishak keep the auction money I should have been paid for the Arabs and the Dutchman in exchange for his silence.

Well, not quite penniless. He did pay me two hundred dollars for presiding at the ceremony that wed him, once and forever, to Caesare Tobur, alias Winston Riles, alias Hans Gerber, alias Horst Brokow, alias the Dutchman. It may have been a little irregular, but I did my usual heart-rending job. At least, I don't recall ever seeing any bride cry and carry on quite as much as the Dutchman did.

5. THE MUMMY

There are worse things than being in Cairo in the summer.
    You can, for example, be in Cairo in the summer with no money, no food, no friends, one suit of clothes, and a crazy Dutchman spreading vile and terrible lies about you to anyone who will listen.
    Or you can be in Cairo in the summer with no money, no food, no friends, one suit of clothes, a crazy Dutchman spreading vile and terrible lies about you to anyone who will listen, and be stalked down a lonely alleyway by a tall dark figure that keeps just out of sight.
    Which I was.
    In point of fact, the street, which was pretty well lit, was just a few short yards away, but it was presently populated by a trio of young men with whom I had recently indulged in certain games of chance involving laminated cardboard rectangles with interesting and intricate markings on *both* sides. Not wishing to bring up bitter memories, I felt it wise to remain off the beaten track, so to speak, when it suddenly came to my attention that my particular track wasn't quite so unbeaten as I might have wished.
    Every time I took a step so did this shadow behind me, and every time I stopped it stopped too. At first I didn't pay it much attention, since I had nothing anyone could possibly want, but then I got to thinking, and decided that any civilized man might well have something some of these Egyptians might want, if only his shoes.
    Well, this cat-and-mouse business went on for the better part of twenty minutes, at the end of which time I would have traded my

soul for a cold bottle of beer, inasmuch as being stalked through the slums of Cairo is mighty thirsty work, when finally this figure stepped out of the shadows holding a wicked-looking dagger in its hand.

"It's all a mistake!" I hollered, throwing my hands up over my head. "This resemblance between me and Rudolph Valentino is purely superficial! I ain't made away with no Egyptian women that I can recall."

"Aw, goddamnit, it's you!" muttered a deep voice. "What the hell are you doing here at this time of night, Lucifer?"

I edged closer to get a better look. It turned out to be the English-speaking porter.

"Why ain't you back with your tribesmen, hightailing it for Uganda?" I asked when I'd finally recognized him.

"I decided to stay here and seek fame and fortune," he replied, lowering his dagger.

"You expect to find them in an alley at four in the morning?" I asked.

"This wasn't my first choice," he admitted sheepishly. "But did you ever try to rob a bank with only a knife?"

"So why didn't you buy a gun?" I asked with a certain detached curiosity.

"With what?" he demanded. "All I have is this damned loincloth. Lucifer, I'm freezing to death!"

"Well, brother," I told him, "freezing to death is one thing I don't have to worry about."

"No?" he said skeptically.

"No," I assured him. "I'm gonna starve to death long before that."

"Well, sorry to have bothered you," he said, walking off.

"Hold on!" I called after him. "Maybe we ought to pool our resources and form a partnership."

"I don't know about that," he said after some thought. "Your last partner is probably drinking my wife's blood at this very moment."

"But he's happy and well-fed," I pointed out. "You gotta consider exactly who and what my last partner was."

"True," he said slowly. "But none of this poor black heathen crap. We're equal partners or the whole thing's off and I'll probably rob you of your clothes."

"Brother," I said sincerely, "you got me all wrong. The Good Lord explicitly forbids me to take advantage of partners of any race, especially when they got me beat by six inches and a good fifty pounds. By the bye, what's your name?"

"You couldn't pronounce it," he said haughtily.

"Try me," I said.

"Kanchupja," he said.

"That being the case, I will call you Friday," I told him.

He shrugged in assent.

"Friday it is, then," I said. "And now, Friday, my partner and cherished friend, I don't suppose you've got any foodstuffs to toss into our mutual pool of resources?"

He held his naked arms above his near-naked body and turned once around. "Just where do you suppose I'd be hiding them, Lucifer?" he asked.

"Just curious," I said.

"I see that you've got an undershirt and a top shirt on," said Friday. "I don't suppose you'd care to turn one of them over to me?"

"Ain't no sense both of us freezing," I replied. "You ain't using your head at all tonight, Friday. It occurs to me that just based on brainpower alone, a fifty-fifty partnership may not be the most equitable arrangement ever to come down the pike."

"You can be an equal partner or a naked victim," said Friday seriously. "I don't recall offering you a third alternative." He placed his hand meaningfully on the hilt of his dagger.

"Well, partner, as long as you put it that way, I guess everything is settled," I said quickly.

We decided to set off in search of food and clothing. By sunrise we still weren't exactly the best-dressed or fattest men in town, so when a crowd began forming on one of the main thoroughfares, we just naturally followed them, hoping for a handout or two, or at least a couple of bulging and unprotected pockets.

What we found was a caravan filled to the brim with golden statues and other baubles, all of them worth a pretty penny or two. Some fellow in khaki shorts and shirt and an oversized pith helmet was standing next to all this stuff, answering questions that a bunch of reporters was tossing up at him.

"What seems to be causing all the commotion, brother?" I asked a European who was standing on the outskirts of the crowd, trying to get a peek of the goings-on.

"Why, don't you ever read a newspaper, friend?" he replied. "This is the first load of treasure to be removed from King Tut's tomb."

"And where might I find this King Tut?" I asked, figuring that any king who gave away gold in such quantities ought to have a little food and a couple of suits left over for a young and modest Christian gentleman who had just undergone months of privation on the Dark Continent.

"I guess you don't read the papers at that!" laughed the European. "King Tutankhamen has been dead for more than three thousand years."

"Just settling the estate now, are they?" I asked, not wishing to appear unduly ignorant.

My companion shook his head with a smile. "King Tut's tomb was discovered on December 1 of last year by an Englishman named Lord Carnarvon and an American named Carter. It's the greatest archaeological find in history."

"Yeah?" I replied. "What all did they find?"

"All kinds of antiques: gilt couches and alabaster vases covered with hieroglyphics. And of course they found Tut himself, the boy king who had been buried with all these marvels millennia ago."

"So now that they found all this stuff, who are they going to sell it to?" I asked.

"Sell it?" He looked horrified. "My good man, all of these fabulous items from antiquity will be put on public display." He looked long and hard at me, and then added: "Under extremely heavy guard, of course."

"Of course," I agreed, nodding my head thoughtfully. "And what about old Tut himself? They gonna finally give him a decent Christian burial?"

"You must be mad!" thundered the European. "Tut is the greatest find of all! They'll be displaying his mummy all over the world."

"You mean to tell me, brother, that they're going to take this dead little boy all wrapped up in bandages and put him on display?" I exclaimed. "Why, it's uncivilized!"

"They're considering bids from various countries right this moment," said my companion.

"Bids? Why would a country pay good coin of the realm to put a mummy on display?"

"They'll charge tourists and recoup their money, never fear," he replied. "But they'll be doing it for the prestige. The profits will be merely incidental."

I thanked him for all this information and moseyed on back to Friday, who had been busy relieving onlookers of their excess change while they were watching the caravan.

"Look, Lucifer," he said, holding up a wad of pound notes. "At least we won't freeze or starve."

"The possibility ain't never crossed my mind," I said, looking around for a store that sold notions and similar goods. "But better still, I think I have hit upon our first business venture."

"First let me get something to wear," said Friday, heading off toward a nearby haberdashery.

I grabbed his arm, hooking it in my own, and kept walking. "Coals to Newcastle," I said. "I'm going to dress you from head to toe."

"What are you talking about?" demanded Friday, with a suspicious look on his face.

"Brother Friday, just put yourself and your economic future in my hands," I said reassuringly. "I promise that by nightfall you'll be the warmest man in all Egypt."

"This isn't going to hurt, is it?" he asked warily.

"Not a bit, Brother Friday."

"You're sure?" he persisted.

"Brother, the only thing that's getting hurt around here is my feelings when I see this lack of trust on your face," I told him. "Now let's get to work."

We began by hunting up a notions shop and buying a couple of hundred feet of bright white bandages. Then we found a little storefront smack-dab in the middle of the Avenue of the Pharaohs and plunked down a pound for a week's rent.

"Now what?" asked Friday as we unloaded our bandages into the empty store.

"Now you take a few shillings," I said, "and go out shopping for a couple of pieces of white cardboard and a can of paint."

"And what will you be doing?"

"Friday, you are the most suspicious partner a mortal man ever did have!" I complained. "I'm just going out to do a little serious thinking. I keep feeling that we need a little something else, but I can't quite put my finger on what it is."

He muttered some gibberish in Swahili and stalked off to make his purchases, while I, deciding that I could think better on my feet than sitting in the store, began walking up and down the winding streets of Cairo. I guess I had gone about half a mile when a small but very rounded figure shot out of a doorway and grabbed me by the hand.

"I have lost my heart to you, noble sir!" she breathed, her dark eyes shimmering above the veil that obscured the rest of her face—and suddenly it dawned on me exactly what our little business venture was lacking.

"It ain't nothing to be ashamed of," I admitted, smiling down at her. "Lots of ladies have felt even stronger emotions on less notice, me being a Christian and a gentleman, and an American to boot."

"I am overcome by an all-pervading desire to give of myself freely to you!" she whispered.

"Freely, you say?" I repeated, as she began leading me into the doorway from which she had emerged.

"Well," she said, modestly dropping her gaze, "there is a small handling and cover charge. As well as an entertainment tax."

"Sister," I said, still smiling at her, "I have a feeling that you and me were meant for each other."

"Good," she said, and from the way her eyes kind of crinkled up at the corners I knew she was returning my grin. "Shall we get the crass commercial details over with?"

"Suits me fine," I agreed. "Of course, I ain't got any money, but . . ."

"Oh, damn!" she snapped, stamping her little foot in rage. "Not another one!"

"I do have a counteroffer to make, though," I said.

"Forget it," she said. "Why don't you go back to sweeping them off their feet in Peoria or Biloxi or some other backwater where paupers can—"

"Where'd you ever hear of them places?" I interrupted.

"Where do you suppose?" she said, ripping the veil from her face.

"Why, you're a white woman!" I exclaimed. "What in blazes are you doing here?"

"I'm an entertainer."

"I can see that," I said admiringly.

"I mean a nightclub entertainer."

"Then how—?" I began.

"There are only two nightclubs in town," she explained. "I played for a week in each. That made me about a tenth of what I need to get back home. And now," she added, putting her veil back over her face, "if you'll excuse me, I've got to get back to work."

"You sure you wouldn't like me to take you away from all this?" I asked.

"What are you talking about?"

"I told you: I've got a little business proposition to make," I said.

"Listen, mister," she said, putting her hands on her hips, "I may not be the most expensive girl in Cairo, but on the other hand you've already admitted that you don't have a penny to your name. What do you intend to pay me with?"

"One-third," I said smiling.

"One-third of what?" she demanded.

"One-third of the stock, of course."

"What stock are you talking about?" she said.

"The stock in our little company," I replied. "Think it over. It's nice, safe, indoor work, and you can keep on your feet."

"Just what kind of scam do you have going?" she asked suddenly, with just a trace of professional curiosity.

"That's a word I am unfamiliar with," I said, "but I have the distinct impression that if I understood it I would be very sorry that I had opened my heart to you, Miss . . . ah, I didn't quite catch your name?"

"Rosepetal," she said. "Rosepetal Schultz. And no snickering."

"The thought never crossed my mind," I replied. "And I am the Right Reverend Doctor Lucifer Jones, pastor of the Tabernacle of Saint Luke."

"Really?" she said dubiously. "You're not just some religious nut who's going to dress me up like a nun and then make vile suggestions?"

"Of course not!" I said. "This is strictly business. Let us proceed to our corporate headquarters on the Avenue of the Pharaohs, where I shall introduce you to our silent partner."

"We have a silent partner?" asked Rosepetal.

"Not at the moment," I admitted. "But by tonight he will be."

We kept walking, talking about this and that and the next thing, and before too long we arrived at the store just as Friday was returning with his purchases.

"Well, hello!" he said, his face lighting up.

"Friday, this is Rosepetal, our new partner," I told him.

"I don't know what Lucifer has in mind for you, but I'm all for it!" he enthused. Then he turned to me. "What do you want me to do with all this stuff I bought?"

"Start painting signs," I said.

"What kind of signs?" he asked.

"Oh, signs that tell all and sundry that the mummy of . . . Rosepetal, name a Pharaoh."

"How about Tutankhamen?" she suggested.

"No. He's been used," I said. "Try a different one."

"Amenophis III is the only other one I know," she said. "Although I suppose there must have been an Amenophis I and II."

I turned back to Friday. "Have the signs say that the mummy of Amenophis III will be on display from six in the evening until midnight at, oh, three shillings per customer."

"I'll have to get a paintbrush," said Friday.

"Do that," I said. "And buy yourself a big dinner. Charge it to the company. And Friday . . ."

He stopped in the doorway. "Yes?"

"I wouldn't drink too much coffee if I were you," I said.

"Lucifer," he said, "I hope you don't think that I'm going to let you wrap me up as a mummy!"

"Perish the thought," I said reassuringly.

He stared long and hard at me again and then left.

"If he's not going to be the mummy, who is?" asked Rosepetal.

"Who says he's not going to be the mummy?"

"But you told him . . . ." she began.

"I told him not to think about it," I replied. "Good advice, too: It would only depress him. And now, if you'll excuse me for an hour or so, I have to do a little shopping. Why don't you make yourself at home and sort of tidy things up a bit?"

Within the next hour I had bought a dilapidated wooden coffin and a batch of gold foil paper and had them both sent right to the store. I picked up a couple of things for Rosepetal and then returned. Friday had finished painting the signs, and was already at work coating the coffin with the gold foil. I had Rosepetal help me hang the signs, and then we settled back to await late afternoon. There being nothing better to do to pass the time of day, I spent our remaining pound on three bottles of inexpensive but explosive vodka, and saw to it that most of the contents were poured down Friday's massive and eager gullet.

When he was properly mummylike in demeanor, which is to say stiff as a board, I carried him to the back room and wrapped him in the bandages, doing his arms and legs separately so he'd be more comfortable, and leaving just a trio of tiny holes for his nostrils and eyes. Then, since his condition hadn't changed appreciably, I had Rosepetal help me heft him over to the coffin, which was standing upright against a wall. We maneuvered him into it and then turned it away from the front window so passersby couldn't get any free looks.

"Thanks!" I panted. "I couldn't have done it without you."

"That's the whole of it?" she said dubiously. "That's all I have to do for a third of the profits?"

"Almost all," I said. "The rest should be a piece of cake."

"The rest?" she said quickly. "What rest?"

"Here," I said, withdrawing a small package I had kept in my pocket since returning. "Why don't you go into the back room and change into this?"

"What is it?" she asked.

"Your costume," I said.

"What costume are you talking about?"

"Look," I said calmly. "Friday's going to bring in all the mummy buffs in the city, but let's be honest: How the hell many of them can there be? Your job is to attract those customers who have absolutely no interest in mummies."

She looked into the bag. "But there's nothing here!" she protested. "Just a necklace and a tiny little G-string!"

"What do you mean, nothing?" I said sharply. "I'll have you know that necklace alone cost me four shillings."

"But Lucifer, I can't wear this! It's indecent!"

"A third of the profits," I said.

"Never! I just couldn't!"

"Must be seven, eight thousand people pass here every night," I said. "At three shillings a head."

"Be quiet!"

"We'll each get a shilling apiece for every man, woman, and child who walks through the door."

She grabbed the bag and stalked off to the back room. "But I think you're a low, despicable con man!" she yelled back over her shoulder.

I looked out the window, checked the sun, and reckoned that it was about a quarter to six, so I set up a table with a little cardboard cash box right by the doorway, pulled a chair over to it, and got ready to unlock the door.

"Is anyone out there with you?" called Rosepetal.

"I'm all alone," I said.

"You're sure?"

"Positive."

She walked out hesitantly, an absolutely gorgeous vision of a full-breasted, narrow-waisted, hot-blooded Egyptian princess. She had her hands crossed modestly in front of her, and kept peeking around to make sure I hadn't lied to her about being alone.

"I feel not unlike a fool in this getup," she said.

"Nonsense!" I said enthusiastically. "You'll outdraw Friday fifty to one."

"You bought the G-string in sort of a hurry, didn't you?" said Rosepetal.

"I didn't spend long hours agonizing over which one to purchase, if that's what you mean," I replied, staring in rapt attention as she inhaled and kind of fluttered all at the same time.

"That's what I mean," she said. "You know, Lucifer, even if the queens and princesses of ancient Egypt walked around in G- strings, which I for one am inclined to doubt, I nonetheless think it very unlikely that their G-strings possessed emblems of Buster Brown and his dog Tyge!"

She spread her hands, revealing the problem.

"So we'll say it's young King Tut and his pet dog," I said quickly. "Who'll know the difference?"

"It's bad enough that I'm out here being a bare-breasted and bare-assed and bare-whatevered shill for you!" she snapped. "I don't intend to be an object of ridicule as well!"

"You just keep on breathing and making muscles like that and I guarantee there ain't nobody going to be laughing at you," I said devoutly. "Now get in the window and start attracting attention. It's time to open for business."

"Couldn't you at least have gotten one with Teddy Roosevelt?" she said, taking her place and starting to gyrate for the pedestrians. "And what about a headdress? Egyptian queens wore headdresses."

"They also didn't chew gum," I said, gesturing for her to empty her mouth. "Now let's just concentrate on business."

So we did, and business concentrated right back on Rosepetal and Friday—mostly Rosepetal—and by seven o'clock we had taken in almost five hundred shillings, and Rosepetal was so tired from shimmying that she forgot all about being embarrassed. Her body glistened with sweat, but I decided not to give her a towel, since it looked for all the world like she had anointed herself with various kinds of ancient Egyptian oils and love potions and stuff like that, and I even added that fact to my spiel.

We kept up our little show for hours, Rosepetal wiggling and wriggling, me telling the customers what remarkable curiosities they were looking at, and Friday mummying it up like he'd been doing it all his life. In fact, I was giving serious thought to franchising the operation when a small, skinny little Englishman with a daintily manicured mustache walked up to me, hat in hand, and cleared his throat.

I stopped my complicated explanation of the Dance of Sublime Surrender, which Rosepetal was right in the middle of, and turned to him.

"Yes, brother," I said, putting on my best Sunday smile. "What can I do for you?"

"I don't mean to interrupt your show," he said apologetically, "or to intrude in matters that are none of my business, but . . ."

"Just spit it right out, brother," I told him. "Don't mind interrupting Queen Cleopatra here; she'll just put everything into a holding pattern until we can get back to her."

"Well, I was looking at the mummy of Amenophis here," said the Englishman, "when the strangest thing happened."

"Oh?" I said. "And what was that?"

"It winked at me."

A woman in the audience screamed.

"I thought it distinctly odd myself," agreed the Englishman, turning to her.

"It must be your imagination," I said smoothly. "Mummies don't wink. And even if they did, a vigorous, manly mummy like this one would wink at *her*"—I gestured toward Rosepetal— "long before he'd think of winking at you."

Suddenly Friday grunted, and three women fainted.

"My God, he's coming to life!" cried an Egyptian.

Friday shook his head, trying to get the tape off his mouth, and stared at me blearily.

"*Frmmx fblimm!*" he said through the bandage.

"He's speaking in the ancient tongue!" cried a woman.

The Egyptians in the crowd started muttering quick little prayers to Amen-Ra, just to be on the safe side. Then Friday gingerly moved a hand to his head, and a couple of pistols appeared.

"Don't waste your bullets, men!" I cried hastily. "He's *already* dead!"

With that, two-thirds of our customers raced for the door. The rest just lay quiet and peaceful on the floor where they had fallen.

Friday must have been nursing a pretty large hangover, because he just stood there in his coffin moaning and gently rubbing his eyes. Finally he saw me, took a step out of the wooden box, and tripped over a couple of bodies, falling smack-dab on his head with a thud so loud it sounded like unto a gunshot. Rosepetal ran over to him, knelt down on the floor beside him, and cradled his head in her lap, stroking it gently. I got a knife and cut a little tape away from his mouth so he could breathe a mite easier, without cutting so much that he couldn't go back to work once we got him back into his box.

It took him about ten minutes to open his eyes. Then he stared straight up at Rosepetal's breasts for another five minutes before he turned his head to me, blinked a couple of times, and struggled to his feet.

"How are you feeling?" I asked, offering him a cup of vodka. "Ready to go back into your tomb?"

He slapped the cup out of my hand and glowered at me—as much as a mummy *can* glower, anyway.

"Who are you that dares address Amenophis?" he rumbled. "I have lain in my crypt for centuries. I will not return to it!"

"If you think acting like this is going to get you out of playing the mummy, Friday, you got another think coming!" I snapped. "Now get on back into the coffin before some of these people littering the floor start waking up!"

I grabbed his arm to lead him back, but he threw me against the wall with no apparent effort.

"Rash mortal!" he bellowed. "The person of Amenophis is sacrosanct!" He reached a bandaged hand out for Rosepetal. "Come, my princess."

"Lucifer, do something!" she whispered as he approached her.

"I'll do something, all right!" I snapped, getting up and dusting myself off. "I'll fire the son of a bitch!"

"Look at his head!" she said, backing away from him. "It's all bloody. Maybe he really does think he's Amenophis!"

Friday caught her and hoisted her over his shoulder.

"*Lucifer!*" she screamed.

I noticed that she wasn't so all-fired terror-stricken that she didn't think to grab the money and stuff it into her G-string as Friday carried her through the doorway and off into the night, so I had no choice but to follow them, though at a respectful distance. We made an interesting sight, what with Friday wandering aimlessly with his half-naked princess slung over his shoulder, Rosepetal frightening everyone away with her screaming, and me tagging along in their wake, trying to figure out how to stop him, if not permanently then at least long enough to get the money back.

He made a couple of quick turns and I momentarily lost sight of him, so I increased my pace. As I rounded the second corner I ran headfirst into a policeman.

"Excuse me, officer," I said.

"Quite all right," he replied.

"Beautiful night, isn't it?" I said.

"Could be a tad cooler, though," he responded thoughtfully.

"By the way, I know it may sound a little peculiar," I said, "but did a half-crazed mummy carrying a naked girl happen to pass by here recently?"

"As a matter of fact, he did," said the officer. "It was most amusing."

"Well, it might have been a lot of things," I said, "but somehow I never thought of amusing as one of them. Didn't you hear her calling for help?"

"Indeed," he said, smiling. "And most convincing it was, too."

"Then why didn't you help her?"

"I just assumed they were advertising a new restaurant or nightclub or something," said the policeman.

"I'm afraid not," I said.

"A new movie, then?"

"No."

"You *will* tell me when I'm getting warm, won't you?" he asked.

"I know it sounds a bit odd," I said, "but they were exactly what they seemed to be."

"You P.R. types have a marvelous sense of humor!" he guffawed. "Tell the truth now: Was it a new Turkish bathhouse?"

I told him he was right, bade him goodnight, and continued my search alone. I must have walked four miles up and down Cairo's winding streets and back alleys when I finally saw this bandaged figure sitting morosely on the sidewalk, his head buried in his hands. I approached him kind of cautiously, inasmuch as he hadn't been all that friendly since falling on his head.

He looked up when I got within a few yards of him, but made no attempt to rise to his feet.

"Well?" I said.

"What do you want, mortal?" he said glumly.

"Where is she?" I demanded.

"Gone," he moaned.

"What the hell do you mean, gone?" I exploded. "She's got all our money."

"Money?" he said dazedly. "What is money?"

"Money is what's ours that she's run off with!" I yelled. "Now where the hell is she?"

"She's all alone, her lithe, youthful body exposed to the elements."

"Her lithe, youthful body can damned well take care of itself just fine!" I snapped. "What direction did it run off in?"

He belched. "You wouldn't know where I could get a fatted calf or something like that, would you?" he asked apologetically. "Ordinarily I would not ask favors of a mere mortal, but I haven't eaten in more than three thousand years, and I'm hungry."

"First the girl, then the food," I said.

"She started pounding on my head," he said, "and when I set her down for a moment she ran into the alleyway." He pointed to a narrow channel between two buildings.

"Then I'd better get after her right quick," I said, starting off.

"Wait!" he cried. "You're not going to leave me here, are you? I mean, everything's changed so much in three thousand years. I have dim, distant memories of sitting around a campfire eating antelope and gallivanting with Nubian maidens. I'm having serious problems adjusting to present-day Egypt."

He looked so unhappy that I finally agreed to let him tag along, and off we went in pursuit of his lost love and my lost money. Gradually the alley turned into a minor street and then a major thoroughfare, but it remained just as empty, probably because when people got a gander at Friday they just naturally remembered that they had urgent business elsewhere.

We finally came to one house that was all lit up like a Christmas tree, and since no one answered when we knocked at the door, we moseyed around back and found ourselves in the midst of a garden party. I could see that Friday was likely to prove a considerable social hazard, because the second he rounded the corner of the house everyone lit out for the hills except for two bearded men who immediately fell to arguing amongst themselves as to whether he was from the Ninth or the Eleventh Dynasty. When Friday helpfully put in that he was Amenophis III, they both turned on him and told him not to interrupt in matters that he knew nothing about.

"But I *am* Amenophis!" he protested.

"What the hell do you know about it?" demanded the smaller of the two men. "That would date you much too late. From the style of your leg bandages, you're much more likely to be Userkaf or perhaps Sahura."

"No," said Friday firmly. "I'm confused about a lot of things, but if there is one thing I know with absolute certainty, it's that I'm Amenophis III."

"You are, are you?" said the taller one nastily. "Then how come you don't know that Amenophis is merely an Anglicization of Amen-hetep?"

"That's what I said," interjected Friday hastily. "I'm Amen-hetep III. I just used Amenophis to make it easier for you gentlemen."

"So you think the Colossi were set up in your honor, do you?" snarled the smaller man. "You think you're the guy who's credited with building the Temple of Amen-Ra at Karnak?"

"How do I know what I've been credited with?" said Friday. "I've been away."

"Piffle!" snapped the larger of the two men. "Do you hear me? I say *piffle*! You're Ninth Dynasty, and that's all there is to it!"

"Eleventh!" protested the smaller man. "Look at the eyeholes!"

"Age could do that," said his companion. "After all, he's at least four thousand years old."

"Three thousand," said Friday petulantly.

"Keep out of this!" they snapped in unison.

"Excuse me, gentlemen," I said, stepping forward, "but may I interrupt you for just a moment?"

"Are you with the mummy?" asked the smaller man suspiciously.

"In a manner of speaking," I replied.

"Is he Ninth or Eleventh Dynasty?" he asked me.

"Brother, I never discuss politics, religion, or Egyptian dynasties," I said firmly.

"My God!" said the taller man in shocked amazement. "What else is there?"

"Well, for one thing, there's naked white women," I said.

"He's right," nodded the smaller man thoughtfully. "There *is* that."

"Have you happened to see any this evening?" I persisted.

"Any what?"

"Any naked white women."

"I'm afraid not," said the taller man.

"Damn!" muttered Friday.

"I'm terribly sorry," continued the taller man, "but it's really not the sort of thing one might expect to see at a cocktail party for Egyptologists."

"More's the pity," added the smaller man. "But why do you ask?"

"We seem to have misplaced one," I said.

"I didn't know they were that easy to misplace," remarked the taller one thoughtfully.

"She was my beloved," said Friday mournfully.

"Ah!" said the smaller man. "That would be Thi, daughter of Kallimma-Sin."

"Only if you accept his cock-and-bull story about being Amenhetep," pointed out the taller one. "Otherwise, she's probably Nitaqert."

"Nitaqert!" screamed his colleague. "Impossible! You've got the wrong dynasty, the wrong wife, and the wrong color!"

Well, their tempers got to flaring up then, so Friday and I just kind of walked back around to the street and continued on our quest. Friday was about as happy as a lovelorn mummy can be, since he had finally found out his lost love's name, but I was getting more depressed with every passing minute, because the longer it took to hunt Rosepetal down, the more likely it was that she'd be able to find some clothing—and if we couldn't find a naked white woman on the streets of Cairo, our chances of finding a particular clothed one didn't seem all that promising.

"Think, Friday!" I said as we walked up and down the avenues. "Where would she be likely to go?"

"I have no idea," he replied, "and I'll thank you to call me Amenhetep or else risk bringing my godly wrath down upon yourself."

And then it came to me in a flash: If *I* were in Rosepetal's britches (figuratively speaking, you understand) and I had as much dishonestly-come-by money as she did, the first thing I'd want to do would be to leave the country. And, being a white woman, it made sense that she'd wait for the next ship out of here where all the white folks did: at Shepheard's Hotel.

I conveyed this line of insightful reasoning to Friday, who, having nothing better to offer by way of suggestions, decided to accompany me. We reached Shepheard's, which had become a jumping-off place for no end of wealthy tourists, just as the sun was starting to rise, and walked up to the registration desk.

"I don't mean to unduly alarm you, sir," said the concierge, "but are you aware of the fact that there is a rather large mummy following you?"

"Yes, I am," I said. "I wonder if I might see your guest register?"

"It doesn't bother you?" he asked.

"What doesn't?" I asked.

"The mummy."

"Not a bit," I said. "If it disturbs you, I'll have it wait outside."

"That won't be necessary," he said in a resigned tone of voice. "When you've worked this desk as long as I have, a mummy can be a pretty trivial thing, if you know what I mean."

I assured him that I knew exactly what he meant, and began reading the guest book. "I don't find the name I'm looking for here," I said at last, "but the party in question may very well have been traveling incognito. Has anyone checked in during the past two or three hours?"

"Would you have in mind a young lady who gave every appearance of having dressed in rather a hurry?" he asked, raising an eyebrow.

"The very person!" I exclaimed.

"I must say, she has a peculiar notion of incognito," he remarked.

"I'd sort of like to surprise her," I said with a knowing smile. "What room is she in?"

"I'm afraid that releasing room numbers is against the rules of the hotel," he replied stiffly.

"That's a pity," I said, stepping aside as Friday walked forward and grabbed him around the neck. "It seems that strangling concierges isn't against any particular rules that govern the behavior of mummies."

"207!" he gurgled. Friday released him and he slid to the floor behind the counter as we raced to the stairs. A moment later we were standing in front of the door to Room 207. I knocked twice, and heard a familiar voice ask who was there.

"Room service," I said.

Rosepetal opened the door, and I stepped in.

"Why, Lucifer!" she exclaimed, startled. "What a pleasant surprise!"

She was wearing a sporty brown suit with matching shoes, all of which looked mighty expensive. I let out a curse the second I saw them.

"Just how the hell much did those duds cost you?" I demanded.

"Not that much," she said, backing away and shoving a small table between us. "I still had enough left to buy a suitcase and to book passage out of this stupid country."

"You spent it all?" I screamed. "All of it?"

"Well, I *am* fleeing for my life, you know," she said. "I have no intention of being here when—" She let out a little shriek as Friday entered the room. "Oh my God!" she cried. "He's back!"

"My beloved Thi!" he intoned, extending his arms and walking slowly toward her. "I shall take you to wife and together we shall rule my kingdom, bring order out of chaos, and produce many heirs."

"He still thinks he's Amenophis!" she wailed.

"Oh, no, my love," said Friday. "I know now that I am Amen-hetep."

"Your name is Friday!" she said, practically crying. "Now leave me alone or I'll miss my boat!"

"But my beloved Thi!" he said, confused. "Can it be that the passing of the eons has dimmed your memory? I am the Pharaoh of all Egypt!"

"You're not even an Egyptian!" she said desperately. "You're a . . . a Nubian!"

"Impossible!" he scoffed.

"You think not?" she said, walking up to him and avoiding his hand. "Let me try to bring you back to your senses once and for all!"

I positioned myself behind him, ready to race out the door if he got violent, while Rosepetal grabbed the end of a bandage that was coming loose at Friday's waist and began unraveling it. Pretty soon she got the most curious expression on her face, and by the time she had unwrapped the tape down to his thighbones she just quit altogether, staring kind of strangely at what she had uncovered thus far.

"Amen-hetep, dear," she sort of crooned, "can you ever forgive me for doubting you?"

"It is forgotten," he intoned graciously. "And you are still my beloved Thi?"

She took one last look and nodded vigorously.

He reached out and embraced her.

"Lucifer," she said, "you'll find my ticket lying on the nightstand. Take it and leave."

"I'll do no such thing!" I said.

"Lucifer," she said sweetly but firmly, "if you're still in this room in ten seconds I shall ask Amen-hetep, Pharaoh of all Egypt, to execute you as slowly and painfully as possible."

I was on my way down the hall in eight seconds flat, and I heard the door to Room 207 slam shut just as I reached the stairway.

That was the last I ever saw of Rosepetal Schultz or Friday, though she did write me after I had finally established my tabernacle to assure me that there were no hard feelings and that Amen-hetep had certain virtues that were well worth waiting a mere three thousand years for.

As for me, I wound up in Morocco, which was as far as Rosepetal could afford a ticket for, and within a mere fortnight I was holding one of the world's rarest and most valuable treasures in my hand.

It was not, as you shall see, quite as simple as it sounds.

6. A RED-LETTER SCHEME

Casablanca wasn't real popular with tourists and sightseers back in the old days, and I was the only passenger to climb down the gangplank when we docked there. It was so hot and dirty and grubby-looking that I could tell right off why it didn't rank way up there with the Riviera and New Orleans and other places of worldwide renown.

There was a very worried-looking little man waiting on the pier, pacing up and down and working himself into a nervous frenzy. I nodded pleasantly and walked past him, but a minute later he raced after me and grabbed me by the shoulder.

"I beg your pardon, *monsieur*," he said apologetically, "but was there not perhaps a lovely young lady on the ship with you who also planned to disembark at Casablanca?"

"None that I know of, brother," I replied.

"But this is terrible!" he cried.

I shared his sentiments, especially since I could have used a little company during the voyage, but I merely smiled at him and kept walking.

He was back beside me a moment later.

"Her name was Mademoiselle Rosepetal Schultz," he said. "Are you sure you did not meet her on the boat?"

"Rosepetal?" I repeated. "Why didn't you say so in the first place, brother?"

"Then she is on the ship after all?" he asked, looking mighty relieved.

"No," I told him. "As a matter of fact, I used her ticket to get here."

"But this is dreadful!" he wailed. "She wired me yesterday that she would be arriving this afternoon!"

"Something came up very unexpectedly," I told him truthfully. "These things happen."

"But why must they always happen to *me*?" he moaned.

"Try reading a couple of chapters from the Book of David," I said soothingly. "I find it usually settles me down when I've had some bad news."

He raised an eyebrow. "You know a lot about the Bible?" he asked.

"The Right Reverend Honorable Doctor Lucifer Jones at your service," I said, extending my hand.

"Would I be correct in assuming that you have no place to stay?" he asked.

"I've temporarily fallen upon hard times, brother," I admitted. "But I've never lost my faith in the Good Lord, Who I know will provide for me." I stared at him curiously. "What did you have in mind?"

"Room, board, and fifty francs a week," he said.

"Done, brother!" I cried. "By the way, how much is that in real money?"

Well, it came to about ten dollars, which isn't a hell of a lot unless the economy happens to be in the midst of a depression—and since that was exactly the state my personal economy was in, I decided to take it unless and until something better turned up.

My employer's name was Andre Peugeot, and in all my born days I never saw a man with more nervous tics and gestures. All he would tell me about his place of business was that it was called Bousbir, and he seemed absolutely flabbergasted when I told him I'd never heard of it.

When we arrived, I was pretty flabbergasted myself to find that something like the Bousbir had escaped my attention, because what it was was the biggest whorehouse in the whole wide world. At least, that's what Andre told me. All I knew for sure is that it was the biggest one I had ever seen, and took up about twice as much space as the Banque de Casablanca, which was right across the street from it.

We walked through a series of lobbies and lounges, each covered with plush carpets and velvet wallpaper and containing as tasty an assortment of fine-looking ladies as ever I did see, until we finally reached a small room with a single bed and a sink and toilet in the corner.

"Your room," said Andre.

"Brother Andre," I said, "we'd better get a couple of things straight right off the bat. I'm pretty liberal as men of the cloth go . . ."

"So I noticed," he said dryly.

"Neverthegoddamless," I continued, "there are some things that are specifically frowned upon by the Good Book, the law, and various other official governing bodies, most of them pertaining to your male customers, that I am not prepared to do even for money, and especially not for a lousy fifty francs a week."

"I quite understand," said Andre. "It is for your unique qualities as a man of God that I have hired you."

"I reckon you could use one around here, at that," I allowed.

"Indeed," he agreed. "It has been one of our greatest needs up to now."

"Well, Brother Andre," I said, "I'll certainly be glad to bring such comfort as I can to your poor wayward girls in any way that I think will help and uplift them the most."

"I appreciate your offer," he replied, "but I think you misunderstand me. It is not my girls who need your spiritual expertise. Rather, it is my customers."

"Your customers?" I repeated. "Why don't they just go to church?"

"We sell many things here, my friend," said Andre. "But perhaps our most precious commodity is fantasy. Do you begin to understand?"

"Not really," I answered.

"Some of our little pageants need—how shall I put it?— a technical adviser."

"Brother Andre, the light is beginning to dawn," I said, shooting him a great big grin.

"Can you do it?"

"Like shooting fish in a barrel," I assured him. "After all, you're asking me to combine my two favorite vocations. Just leave everything to me and the Good Lord, and I'm sure we'll manage to work things out betwixt us."

Which we did, at least for a few days. But within a week the customers and even the girls were getting a little jaded and began demanding new material, and I took to wandering through the bazaars during the afternoons, searching for ideas that had nothing to do with cardinals and nuns, or black masses, or maniacal rabbis, or secret Chinese fertility ceremonies, or any of the other similarly pedestrian productions I had been directing and coaching.

It was during one such sojourn through the marketplace that I saw a white man who looked vaguely familiar. He had his back to me, and was browsing at a table about fifty feet away, but I couldn't get the thought out of my mind that I knew him from somewhere. I stayed right where I was, pretending to examine some old pottery, until at last he paid for the dates he was munching on and I finally got a look at his face.

It was Erich Von Horst!

Not wishing to cause a scene in public, especially since I didn't speak French or Arabic and I had the feeling that no one around there spoke anything else, I continued to browse until he left the bazaar. Then, being careful to keep out of sight, I followed him for almost a mile until he entered an old, dusty, run-down hotel.

I waited five minutes, then entered it. There was no desk clerk on duty, so I reached over the counter, grabbed hold of the registration book, and began looking at it. There was no Von Horst listed, nor even a Captain Peter Clarke, but it didn't matter: a gentleman named Fritz Wallensack was the only guest currently in residence. I tiptoed up to his room, threw the door open, and walked in.

"Von Horst!" I bellowed. "You owe me two thousand and forty English pounds!"

"Why, Doctor Jones," he said, looking up from his bed, where he was lying with his head propped up against the moldy wall. "How very nice to see you again. Have you been in Casablanca long?"

"Don't give me that crap, Von Horst!" I snapped. "I want my money!"

"I don't doubt it," he chuckled.

"Well?" I demanded.

"If I had your money, or indeed if I had *anybody's* money, do you think I'd be staying in a place like this?" he said calmly. "You're welcome to search the premises, of course, but I can guarantee that you won't find anything except an exceptionally dirty shirt and a pair of socks with holes in them."

"What about my money?"

"It was well spent," he assured me with a smile. "You'd have enjoyed every shilling of it had you been in my place."

"I wasn't in your goddamned place!"

"Well, yes, I was rather afraid you'd look at it that way," he sighed.

"Just how soon do you intend to make restitution, realizing of course that I'm going to be your constant companion until that happy moment occurs?" I said.

"As soon as I can work out a few unpleasant details I'll be happy to pay you back, and with interest," said Von Horst.

"What details?" I demanded.

"My dear fellow, I hope you don't think I'm in Casablanca for my health!"

"Just what *are* you doing here?" I asked suspiciously.

"I've been here for two months, working on the biggest deal of my life," he said, lowering his voice. "But the Casablanca police know who I am, and I haven't been able to make a move without being watched. So here I sit, slowly going broke in this grubby hotel, less than half a mile away from a fortune that I could retire on. And the worst part of it is, there's a time limit on the damned operation! But sooner or later they'll have to relax their vigil, and then . . ." His voice trailed off.

"Just how much is this deal worth?" I asked with as much lack of interest as I could muster on the spur of the moment.

"At least fifty thousand pounds," he said without hesitation.

"That much?"

He nodded—and then he stared at me kind of funnylike for a very long minute.

"I wonder . . ." he said softly, still looking at me.

"About what?" I said.

"You know," he said, more to himself than to me, "it just might work."

"What might?"

"Jones," he said suddenly, "forget about what I owe you. How would you like to make some *real* money?"

"I imagine I could be coerced into it," I admitted.

"Good," he said. "But we'll have to move fast. Can you be ready to leave the country in two or three hours?"

"Ain't nothing around to stop me," I replied.

"Well, Jones," he said, all businesslike, "I'm afraid we're going to have to trust each other, much as I dislike the thought of it. But unfortunately there is no way to avoid giving you the details of the plan. All I can do is assure you that such knowledge will do you absolutely no good without me."

"Shoot," I said.

"Three short blocks from here is a small Christian mission, run by two elderly German sisters and their middle-aged nephew. Inside the mission is a speaker's podium. On a shelf inside the podium is a copy of the Bible." He paused for effect. "Jones, that Bible is a Jacobean Red Letter edition!"

"That's something special?" I asked.

"There were only six printed," he said. "The sisters don't know what it is, so stealing it should present no great difficulty. But the moment I try to leave the country, or even the city, I'm going to be searched six ways to Sunday, and since I am not known as a religious man, sooner or later one of the gendarmes is going to send some telegrams to various religious organizations or antiquarian bookdealers, and then the shit will hit the fan." He smiled. "However, no one will question a man of God who carries a Bible with him. You can walk out with it right under their noses!"

"Sounds good to me, Brother Von Horst," I said.

"You are probably thinking that once I turn the Bible over to you, there is nothing to stop you from selling it and reaping the entire profits for yourself," he continued.

"Such a notion never crossed my mind!" I protested vigorously while crossing my fingers behind my back.

"Well, just in case it does, let me tell you that forty-eight hours from now I intend to send a letter to the Moroccan government telling them what the Jacobean Red Letter Bible is, and grossly exaggerating how much it is worth. They will promptly put out a reward for its return worth considerably more than the book itself, and nine dealers out of ten will be more likely to turn you in for the reward than buy the book from you."

"So where are we going to sell it?" I asked.

"There is an American collector who will be in Algiers exactly seven days from now," said Von Horst. "He knows he'll be purchasing stolen goods, and is willing to run the risk that entails in exchange for getting possession of the Bible. You do not know his name, and he does not know yours. He will buy only from me. Have we got a deal?"

I nodded, and shook his hand on it.

"Good," he said. "I will meet you ten minutes after dark."

"Here?" I asked.

"No. They'll be watching this place." He lowered his head in thought for a moment, then looked up. "Do you know where the Bousbir is?"

"I'm sure I can find it," I replied earnestly.

"First lounge to the right, ten minutes after dark," he said.

I returned to the Bousbir, gave a couple of the girls one last strenuous coaching session, and waited for dark. Von Horst showed up on schedule, panting like he'd been running full speed for a while, and thrust a Bible into my hands.

"That's it!" he said. "Don't try to hide it. Just carry it out in the open and act like it was any other book. I'll be creating a diversion while you escape with it."

"Fine," I said, tucking it under my arm. "When and where do we meet?"

"On the waterfront in Algiers is a tavern known as the Fisherman's Reward. Today is the ninth of August. You must meet me there on the sixteenth of August at precisely one-fifteen p.m. If you come early, you may attract undue attention, and if you're even five minutes late our buyer may lose his nerve and depart. Have you a reliable watch?"

"Not since a little card game I got into in Johannesburg," I admitted.

He pulled a beat-up gold watch out of his pocket and handed it to me. "Take mine," he said. "And try not to gamble it away."

"What's that little thing dangling from the chain?" I asked.

"A rabbit's foot," he answered. "For luck."

"Well, I hope it brings me more luck than it brought the rabbit," I said. "I guess I might as well get started now."

He stuck his head out into the hall, then nodded and gestured that it was clear. A few minutes later I was on the main road out of town, heading toward Algeria.

Just as I reached the outskirts of Casablanca I heard a lot of shooting and sirens and things behind me, but no one bothered me, so I kept right on walking. I stopped in the city of Fez long enough to buy another Bible that looked for all the world just like the Jacobean Red Letter edition, and made it to the Algerian border on the evening of the eleventh. The Moroccan and Algerian border patrols and customs officials searched me up and down and sideways, and spent the better part of an hour jabbering about the tooth of a lion or leopard or something, which made absolutely no sense to me, but they finally let me pass and I bedded down in Algeria.

I hitched a ride on an oxcart into Ouahran and spent a considerable portion of the day exploring the scenic wonders of that exotic city, which didn't look a whole lot different from Casablanca except that it didn't have nothing to compare to the Bousbir. I stopped at the local library just before closing time, found the dustiest, most unused bookshelf in the place, stuck the Jacobean Red Letter Bible up against the wall behind a set of books about French civil law where no one would be able to see it, and continued on my way.

I did a little vigorous preaching the next morning, and so amused a tribe of Berbers that they fed me and let me ride on horseback with them to the outskirts of Algiers, where they pitched their tents. Since I didn't want to show up too early, I spent the next couple of days in the Berbers' camp teaching them a somewhat sporting form of rudimentary statistical analysis having to do with the number twenty-one, and when I finally took my leave of them I took certain fond gold and paper remembrances with me.

I arrived on the waterfront just before noon on the appointed day and quickly spotted the Fisherman's Reward, a seedy-looking dive with a clientele more in need of salvation than most. I spent the next hour walking around the area, checking Von Horst's watch every few minutes, and practically beating off a steady stream of street urchins who all seemed to be business agents for their older sisters.

Finally, at exactly one-fourteen, I walked into the tavern and took a seat at an empty table in the back. Von Horst arrived about a minute later and joined me.

"Have a good trip?" he asked in low tones.

"No problems," I said. "Where's our buyer?"

"He should be here any second," said Von Horst. "He's already put down some earnest money with a confederate of mine."

We ordered a couple of beers and waited in silence. When no one else had walked in by one-thirty, Von Horst went over to the bar and made a quick phone call. He came back to the table looking very upset.

"Louis Blaine has been arrested," he said grimly.

"Our buyer?"

He nodded. "The stupid son of a bitch got drunk last night and took a punch at the Prefect of Police."

"What do we do now?" I asked, starting to feel kind of uneasy around the edges.

"We wait," said Von Horst. "He ought to be out in a couple of weeks, and we'll try to set up another meeting with him. In the meantime, we'll live on his down payment. Have you got the book with you?"

Well, as you can imagine, I wasn't in any hurry to let Von Horst spend two weeks examining the particular Bible I was toting around, so me and the Lord held a quick pow-wow to devise a course of action.

"I don't want to wait," I announced at last. "You know what these jerkwater countries are like. He could be in jail for years."

"There's really no alternative," Von Horst replied. "I wasn't kidding about writing the Moroccan government. Right now that book's too hot to try to sell elsewhere."

"Well, it just don't seem fair that I should be stuck in this hellhole because your buyer went and did something stupid," I said. "After all, I fulfilled *my* part of the bargain."

"I don't know what you expect *me* to do about it," he replied irritably. "I'd pay you if I could, but I don't have the money."

"You've got the down payment," I said. "How much was that?"

"Five thousand pounds," he answered kind of grudgingly.

"That's more than twice what you stole from me back in Dar-es-Salaam," I said. "Give it to me and we'll call things square. I just want to get the hell out."

"It's a deal!" he said enthusiastically. "Let me have the Bible."

"Let me have the money first," I said.

He shrugged, pulled an envelope out of his pocket, and handed it over to me. I opened it, thumbed through the wad of bills, nodded, and stuck it inside my shirt.

"Here it is," I said, pulling the Bible out of my shirt and giving it to him. I held my breath as he gave it a brief look, but it was too dark in the bar for him to notice that it wasn't the Red Letter edition.

"You're crazy, Jones," he said, placing the Bible on the table next to his glass. "Within two weeks, three at the most, he'll be out and you could have had twenty-five thousand pounds."

"The Good Lord frowns on greed," I said piously.

"Oh, I almost forgot," he said. "Could I borrow some money from you, to get me through to . . . ah . . . ?"

"Why not?" I said with a smile, giving him some of my Berber money. "Keep the change."

"Thanks," he said. "It's a pleasure to do business with you, Doctor Jones."

"Same here," I said, rising and shaking his hand.

"By the way," he added, "do you suppose a rich man like yourself would mind giving me my watch back?"

I chuckled, handed it to him, and left the tavern. The second I got out the door I took off like a bat out of hell for the nearest ticket office, booked passage on a boat that was leaving Algiers in ten minutes, paid for it with my Berber winnings so as not to flash the five thousand pounds Von Horst had given me, and raced up the gangplank without being seen.

As soon as we were safely out to sea I hunted up a deckhand and found out that I was aboard *The Dying Quail*, bound for the Cape after going through Gibraltar. It wasn't exactly my first choice of destinations, but with five thousand pounds in my pocket I wasn't too upset about it. And, along with the money, I still had the Red Letter edition of the Bible, which I figured on returning for in a year or two, when the gendarmes were a little less sensitive about such things.

After spending a few minutes walking around the deck convincing everyone that I was perfectly calm and had nothing to hide, I went back to my cabin, locked the door, and pulled out the envelope. As I removed the money prior to putting it in orderly stacks and admiring it a little before dinnertime, a small folded piece of paper fluttered down to the floor.

I picked it up, opened it, and read it as follows:

11th August, 1923

My Dear Doctor Jones:

As you may very well have guessed by now, there is of course no such thing as a Jacobean Bible, let alone a Red Letter edition of it. I apologize for having fooled you, but since you have doubtless hidden it somewhere and substituted another totally worthless Bible in its place, I must confess that I don't feel quite as guilty as I otherwise might.

This entire affair began when I first saw you back in Casablanca. I was under constant surveillance by the local police—that much, at least, was true—and I needed an accomplice who could take something out of the country for me. You really are not the most observant person I have ever encountered; I must have wasted five afternoons in that incredibly boring marketplace before you finally recognized me—and even then I almost lost you a couple of times while you were shadowing me back to my hotel.

If you have read this far you have doubtless figured out that there never was a Louis Blaine. He is, of course, one of my professional identities, and I hereby will him to you, to use whenever you wish. He was, however, absolutely essential to the success of this operation, for without him you would have had no reason to show up at precisely one-fifteen, and thus I would have had no reason to give you my watch. Hidden in the rabbit's foot is the Lion's Tooth, the largest and most valuable diamond in Africa. I thank you for delivering it in such excellent condition.

If you are reading this for the first time, I must assume that you have not yet spent any of the five thousand pounds I allowed you to swindle me out of. My advice to you is that if you must spend them you do so very carefully, as the print job is of an inferior grade and they are worth, if anything, even less than the Bible.

Your obedient servant,
Erich Von Horst

About ten seconds after I put the letter down I got violently seasick for the first time in my life.

7. MUTINY

The Dying Quail didn't have much in the way of a passenger list, but on the other hand *The Dying Quail* wasn't all that much of a ship, so things kind of worked out even. I had heard that shipboard romances could be really memorable occurrences, but the only person who I could find on deck at night was a wrinkled old dermatologist from Korea who spent the better part of a week trying to convince me that contrary to popular belief the earth was really flat, or at the very least built along the lines of a gently pitched roof.

The food was okay if you liked tuna. It was absolutely terrible if you didn't. I didn't, and by the third or fourth day out of port, I don't think anybody else did either.

There was an elderly English couple who had just bought a cattle farm in the Transvaal area and spent most of their time fighting about whether to butcher them all on the spot or maybe get a little milk from them first. There was a scrawny blond Swede who never left his cabin except to eat tuna and then get rid of it over the side of the boat. There was a trio of German girls, round and firm and much too fully packed, who didn't speak a word of any civilized tongue and spent all their time taking pictures, not that the water off the Ivory Coast looked all that different from the water next to Liberia. There were a couple of East Indian men who would strip off all their clothes every morning, sit in the blazing sun all day with their legs crossed kind of painful-like, tell everybody not to eat hamburgers, and then go back to their rooms as soon as it was dark. We had a down-on-his-luck actor from Canada who kept reciting the more obscure soliloquies from *Troilus and Cressida*, and a writer from Paraguay who drank in most of his local color from a bottle of Scotch. And, finally, we had a stunningly beautiful belly dancer from Greece who apologized for distracting us but explained that she had to sunbathe in the nude because her audiences didn't like to see different shadings where various straps had been. Watching her body get an even tan was about as quick-moving a spectator sport as watching paint dry, but it did hold certain advantages over paint-watching when viewed in all of its many aspects, and it provided me with just about my only form of diversion during the first week of the voyage.

The captain and the crew were nominally British, but I don't think more than half of them had ever gotten to within five hundred miles of London or Liverpool. The rest were swarthy, unwashed seamen who swore in Slavic tongues and spent a lot of time glaring sullenly at the passengers, who either ignored them or lectured them on the evils of eating beef. The captain himself was a jovial, balding little man with a red mustache, white knee-length shorts, a huge belly, and a driving urge for perfection that caused him to tell a joke thirty or forty times until he got it right.

It was on our eighth day out of Algiers that the captain, whose name was Roberts, announced that he was sick and tired of talking to the crew and would be interested in picking up the gauntlet of any passenger who might care to challenge him to a game or two of chance. Well, the Indians probably couldn't have uncrossed their legs even if they'd wanted to, and the belly dancer was busy soaking up the sun, and the writer was too drunk, and the German girls couldn't understand him, and most of the other passengers were otherwise occupied, which meant that a few minutes later Captain Roberts and I were sitting across a table from one another, *mano a mano*, preparing for a little contest of skill involving a small stack of colorful pasteboards.

The Good Lord must have had His attention diverted elsewhere—probably He was making sure that the belly dancer got tan everywhere she wanted to, for which I couldn't blame Him none—because He wasn't breathing hard over my shoulder. I lost almost three thousand pounds, the only saving grace being that the money itself probably wasn't worth a whole lot more than the cards.

Captain Roberts didn't seem to notice the difference in the notes, though, or else he may have decided that it was simply a normal variation, because he pocketed the money and announced to passengers and crew alike that he was now at peace with the world and would be breaking out a case of his second-finest drinking stuff for dinner at no extra cost, or at most a very nominal one.

I think it would be a fair assessment to say that we all enjoyed the evening meal. Everyone partook heavily of the captain's liquor, it being the only alternative to eating still more tuna. After the last bottle was drained, and the belly dancer had gone off with the actor, and the three German girls were getting kind of chummy with the crew, and the writer and the Korean dermatologist were coming close to blows about whether the world was flat or merely slanted, those of us who remained finally bade each other a fond goodnight and went off to our various cabins.

I woke up with a start a couple of hours later when I heard a scream and a splash in quick succession. It took me just a minute to climb into my duds and get out on deck, where I found a couple of the English crewmen looking over the side of the boat.

"Good evening, brothers," I said. "Either of you two hear something sort of unusual in the last couple of minutes?"

"Can't say as to how we have, sir," said one of them.

"*Help!*" cried a voice that seemed to be coming from a considerable distance away.

"There it is again!" I said. "You *sure* you don't hear something strange?"

"That's just Captain Roberts hollering for help, sir," said the second crewman soothingly. "Nothing peculiar about that at all, seeing as how we dumped him overboard and left him in our wake."

"Do you fellows have any special reason for what, on the surface of it, seems an act sadly lacking in Christian charity?" I asked them.

"Reason enough!" snapped the first crewman. "We all got together for a little game of cards after the party broke up, and he wound up the big loser."

"So?" I asked.

"The blighter paid us off with bogus money!" said the crewman.

"No!" I exclaimed. "And he seemed like such a nice, friendly fellow when I played with him this afternoon."

"Did you win or lose, sir?"

"Oh, I won a couple of thousand pounds," I said, pulling out the last of Von Horst's money and handing it over to them. "Is it any good?"

"Maybe for lighting cigars with," said one of them disgustedly. "Certainly not for spending. I'm sorry to be the one to tell you, sir."

"Dangblast it!" I swore bitterly. "And he appeared to be such a decent, Christian sort of man, if you know what I mean. Seems a shame to drown him."

"Oh, he isn't going to drown, sir," said one of the crewmen.

"He ain't?" I said, startled. "Why the hell not?"

"We tossed him a couple of life preservers, and we're only a mile off the coast. He'll make it ashore, all right."

"But he definitely won't be coming back aboard ship?" I asked.

"No, sir."

"Serves you right, you scoundrel!" I cried, shaking my fist over the side of the ship. "That'll teach you to cheat a man of God!"

"Being as how you're a man of God and all, sir," said one of the crewmen, "I wonder if you could help us with a slight moral dilemma in which we find ourselves."

"Certainly, my good man," I said. "What seems to be the problem?"

"While we don't feel particularly mutinous," he began, "what we done *could* be misconstrued as mutiny by certain admiralty courts and various other powers of the high seas."

"And you'd like me to testify on your behalf, is that it?" I asked.

"Oh, no, sir," said the other. "We wouldn't dream of imposing upon you like that."

"What exactly do you want me to do, then?" I asked.

"Well, sir," said the first crewman, "it would go very hard with us, very hard indeed, sir, if it looked like we tossed old Captain Roberts overboard so that we could wrest control of the ship from him, to seize power as it were."

"Yeah, I can see where that might put a little crimp or two in your defense," I agreed.

"So we was wondering, sir, if you'd be good enough to take over as captain until we get to the Cape?"

"Me?" I exclaimed.

"Not to worry, sir," he said. "We'll run the ship for you, and do the navigation, and feed the customers (provided they like tuna) and keep the decks scrubbed down, and make sure everything is ship-shape. But what with you being a man of God and all, it won't go so hard on us when Captain Roberts finally reaches civilization and institutes legal action against us."

"Which he may never do," added the other. "It being such a dark and moonless night, he could hardly be sure who it was that pushed him overboard. Or he could die of pneumonia, or of being et by sharks, or any one of a number of similar tragedies could befall him, sir."

"Sad," agreed the first crewman, nodding his head.

"Indeed," said the second.

"I'll do it!" I said at last. "After all, while I been captain of my own soul on its long and heartrending journey through life, I ain't never been captain of a ship before. I might just learn something."

"Also," noted the first crewman, "the captain gets to eat steak."

"That little fact ain't exactly escaped my attention," I said with a smile. "Well, as long as I got you two to thank, I guess you'll be serving as my executive officers. What are your names?"

"Call me Ishmael," said the first. "Ishmael Bledsoe."

"And I'm Luthor Christian." replied the second.

"Fine," I said. "And you can call me Captain Jones."

"We'll be happy to, Captain Jones, sir," said Ishmael. "But there may be some amongst our crew—the rowdier elements, you understand—who may not be so inclined."

"We'll incline 'em against the mainmast for a few days," I said. "That ought to assuage their doubts."

"I regret to point out that we don't have a mainmast, Captain Jones," said Luthor apologetically.

"Some of them," continued Ishmael, "might even wonder what right we had to throw Captain Roberts overboard, them not being acquainted with the concept of personal honor and paying one's debts with legal tender and other such rarefied philosophic points."

"No problem at all," I said after a moment's thought. "Mr. Christian?"

"Yes, sir?"

"Give the signal to abandon ship," I said.

"You're the captain," he shrugged, and went off to the bridge. A moment later a loud, raucous siren had awakened everyone on board.

"Why don't you go make sure everyone has a life preserver?" I suggested to Ishmael. "And, in keeping with our personal code of honor, we three will go down with the ship."

He started passing out a batch of little white inner tubes, and within ten minutes everyone except Ishmael, Luthor, and me was in the water.

I picked up a megaphone and held it just in front of my lips.

"Good evening!" I called out. "This is your new captain, Lucifer Jones, speaking. I just want you all to know that this has been one of the better abandon-ship drills that it has ever been my privilege to witness."

I waited for the screams of outrage to die down a little, and then continued.

"I am afraid that poor Captain Roberts found it necessary to abrogate his command. His last wish was that I take over and make sure that *The Dying Quail* completed its voyage in perfect safety. He felt that, as a man of God, I was unquestionably the best qualified among all of us to deal with such problems as might arise. Those of you who share his opinion will be allowed back on board; the rest of you are advised not to splash too violently, as that constitutes just the kind of motion that attracts sharks."

A couple of sharks providentially appeared just then, and within less than three minutes everyone was back on board and I was unanimously acknowledged as the one and only lawful captain, by grace of God and His denizens of the deep.

Well, things went pretty smoothly for the next couple of days, much to my surprise. Nobody seemed to care who was captain as long as they all got to where they were going, and when they heard about how Captain Roberts had reneged on his debts of honor, they actually gave Ishmael and Luthor a standing ovation.

We passed Nigeria and Cameroon without any untoward incidents. Then one morning I strolled out on deck at about noon, having arisen early, and got the shock of my life. Usually we traveled about a mile off the coast to avoid reefs and other menaces to navigation, but now there was a forest about sixty yards off to the left—and as if that weren't enough, there was another one half a mile away on the right.

"Mr. Christian!" I bellowed.

"Sir?" said Luthor, arriving a few seconds later.

"Mr. Christian," I said, "unless the ocean has gotten an awful lot narrower or the ship has gotten an awful lot wider, I am forced to the conclusion that we are no longer on course."

"You noticed, sir," said Luthor noncommittally.

"Of course I noticed!" I yelled. "Little things like losing the Atlantic Ocean don't easily escape my attention. Now where the hell are we?"

"I should have thought that would be obvious, Captain Jones," replied Luthor. "We're on the Congo River."

"What the hell are we doing here?" I persisted.

"Some of our crew members threatened to go on a sit-down strike if they had to keep eating tuna," said Luthor. "Mostly the Slavs, sir; very few of the blueblooded Englishmen."

"Is that all?" I said, relieved. "Just flog 'em and let's get back on course."

"My very thought," said Luthor. "But we do have one little problem, sir."

"Don't worry about legalities, my good man," I said. "A captain's word is law onboard ship."

"That goes without saying," agreed Luthor.

"Oh? Then what's the problem?" I asked him.

"There are a lot more of them than there are of us, and they're bigger."

"Yeah, I can see where that does pose a bit of a problem," I agreed.

"Also, no one who's been eating the tuna right along is in any condition for so strenuous an activity as flogging people, even if the crewmen would stand still for it."

"That being the case, Mr. Christian," I said, "it is my firm conclusion that we should seek out a river and put the ship into it."

"We've done that, sir," he said.

"Good!" I said. "Next, equip a party of Slavic crewmen and send them out to hunt up some meat."

"They're doing that right now, sir," he said.

I couldn't think of any more executive orders, so I dismissed him and took a couple of minutes to examine our surroundings. We had veered a bit closer to the shore, and I could see that it was all covered by trees and vines. It looked hot and full of bugs, and I sure didn't envy the poor men who had to go hunting in there. Everything looked green and damp, which kind of matched the color and texture of the hundred or so crocodiles that were milling around casting hungry glances up toward the boat. Every now and then they'd swim a little too close to a hippo, which sort of reminded me of the Dutchman except that it didn't wear a soiled white suit, and the hippo would just bite one of the crocs in half. It didn't seem to bother the crocodile's friends and relations none, but I noticed that whenever this happened they all kind of moved downstream a little.

Anyway, I got a little tired of looking at all these reptiles and river horses after a while, so I took out Captain Roberts's fishing rod and decided to bag a couple of trout or whatever, but all I kept hooking was crocodiles, so I finally gave it up and went back to my cabin to wait for the hunting party to return, which they did toward late afternoon, and on the run.

I burst out of my door as soon as I heard the rifle shots. Ten crew members were racing for *The Dying Quail* as fast as their lifeboat could go, and behind them, in hot pursuit, were half a dozen war canoes filled with black savages who were waving spears and shooting arrows in their wake.

Ishmael raced to the bridge and saluted.

"What do you want us to do, Captain Jones, sir?" he said.

"I haven't made up my mind yet," I said, squinting at the lifeboat. "Can you see if they actually caught any meat?"

"Too hard to tell from here," said Ishmael.

"Well, I suppose it's our duty to protect 'em," I said. "Fire a broadside at the canoes."

"I'm afraid that's quite impossible, sir," said Ishmael.

"What the hell's the good of being captain if I can't fire a broadside into an enemy every now and then as the mood takes me?" I said, ducking as a couple of arrows flew overhead.

"First of all, we're facing the wrong way to fire a broadside," said Ishmael.

"Then turn us around!" I commanded.

"And second of all," he continued, unperturbed, "we don't have any weapons."

"Why the hell not?" I demanded.

"This is a passenger ship, not a destroyer," he replied, ducking another arrow. "There were only four rifles on board, and all of them are with the hunting party."

"Well, just what *have* we got?" I asked, sidestepping a colorful spear that just missed beheading me.

"There's a rather wicked-looking butcher's knife in the kitchen," he suggested. "And I've heard the actor bragging about his skill at fisticuffs."

"And that's our total offensive and defensive weaponry?" I asked.

He nodded.

"Then wait until our party is back on the ship and let's make tracks out of here," I said.

The hunting party was on deck within thirty seconds, and Ishmael gave the order to turn the ship 180 degrees and then proceed at full speed. The natives increased the intensity of their attack, and began making very rude sounds when they saw we were hightailing it for the open sea.

"Shoal ahead, sir!" cried Luthor.

Ishmael stood at the wheel, which had about a dozen arrows embedded in it, and steered.

"Shoal to starboard, sir!" cried Luthor.

Ishmael ducked a spear and two more arrows and kept steering. Suddenly there was a terrible crunching sound.

"Shoal beneath, sir!" said Luthor.

"I don't suppose we're prepared to repel boarders?" I asked as Ishmael tried to steer the ship and found out that the wheel wouldn't move.

"We're mostly a pleasure ship, sir," he said sadly.

"Maybe if we threw some beads at them, or offered them the belly dancer . . ."

"Millions for defense, but not one cent for tribute!" I bellowed, mostly because beads hadn't accomplished all that much good with the last few tribes I had encountered, and I had other plans in mind for the belly dancer.

"Oh, very well said, sir!" cried Ishmael. "Words to die for!"

"Who said anything about dying?" I replied. "Have we at least got a flare gun aboard, so we can see them better?"

He walked to a nearby cabinet and pulled one out. I took it from him and fired it, illuminating the sky with red-gold streaks of light. Suddenly all the savages started screaming in terror, and a minute later they were prostrating themselves in their boats, a difficult feat of balance even if there hadn't been a couple hundred crocodiles in the water.

"I think the flares have convinced them we're some kind of gods, sir," said Ishmael.

"*We?*" I repeated. "I don't recollect anyone else firing the flares."

"I think the flares have convinced them that you're some kind of god, sir," amended Ishmael.

"I think you may have something there," I said. "Why don't you and Luthor figure out how to get us off this damned shoal while they're busy worshiping me?"

He and Luthor hopped to it, and after about an hour of rocking and lurching, I heard another crunch and suddenly we were moving through the water again. The cheer let out by the crew and passengers was drowned out by the cheer from the savages, who began paddling along in our wake. They were still following us when we hit the ocean and turned left. From time to time one of them would spear a fish and throw it onto our deck as a small tribute, but for the most part they were content to worship me from afar.

The hunting party hadn't managed to bring back any fresh meat. In fact, their first shot had winged one of the natives and precipitated the whole affair of the previous evening. It didn't matter much anyhow; they were so bitten up by bugs that they probably wouldn't have had much stomach for good red meat any time before we hit the Cape.

I posted a new Ship's Regulation to the effect that sunbathing was now allowed only on the captain's private deck. Unfortunately, the belly dancer decided that she was tan enough, and I kept stumbling over the two East Indians every time I went into and out of my cabin until I rescinded the order a couple of days later.

We had no more serious problems until we were almost south of Portuguese West Africa, at which point our Korean dermatologist borrowed one of the rifles, lashed himself to the wheel, and explained that while he had nothing against us personally, we nonetheless had to turn the ship around before we sailed over the edge of the world.

I signaled Luthor and Ishmael to leave me alone on the bridge with him, and the two of us got to talking about one thing and another, and had a friendly little drink to pass the time of day, and I finally convinced him that the edge of the world was somewhere around Brussels, and actually we were going uphill and toward safety. He was one very happy Korean for the rest of the trip, and hardly bothered anyone at all, except for our drunken writer, who was convinced that the edge of the world was more in the neighborhood of Lincoln, Nebraska.

One day, when we had gotten to within a couple of hundred miles of the Cape, the savages who were still behind us and still tossing us an occasional fish or eel began screaming at the tops of their lungs.

"What's the problem now?" I said, coming out of my cabin, where I had been thinking of ways to convince the belly dancer that her tan was fading.

"Whales off the starboard bow, sir," said Luthor.

I looked, and sure enough, there were about twenty of the beasts making toward the ship, flopping and splashing and spraying up huge geysers of water from the tops of their noses, and otherwise looking very ominous.

"Does this kind of thing happen very often, Mr. Christian?" I asked him, looking about for the nearest life preserver.

"Well, that all depends, Captain Jones, sir," he said.

"On what?" I asked.

"On whether we're in port or not, sir," he replied.

"We're on the high seas!" I pointed out to him.

"Well, that does make it more likely, sir," he agreed.

"What do you do when they attack the ship?" I asked.

"Personally, I close my eyes very tightly and pray that they'll go away," said Luthor with obvious sincerity.

"I suppose rifle bullets would just enrage them?" I asked.

"I really have no idea," said Luthor. "You can certainly try rifle bullets if you wish. Personally, I think I'm going to go below and grab a little nap." He raced off before I could order him to remain on duty.

The whales got to within two hundred yards, and our faithful natives suddenly unconverted and headed back toward the mouth of the Congo River, some two thousand miles north of us. The whales ignored them and drew even closer.

"They look hungry," said Ishmael, who had suddenly appeared at my side.

"You ever seen a whale that didn't?" I asked out of curiosity.

"Once," he admitted. "Of course, it was dead."

"Of course," I said. One of the whales got to within about twenty yards and I threw a sextant at it. It bounced off its nose without causing any injury that I could see.

"Do whales eat people?" I asked.

"I imagine whales eat pretty much what they want to," said Ishmael, drawing closer as if for comfort.

"I mean, maybe they'll go away and leave us alone," I said hopefully.

"Maybe," he said doubtfully.

"And maybe," I said, struck by a sudden flash of inspiration, "they're just here to beg at the table."

"What are you talking about, Captain Jones?" said Ishmael.

"Go down to the kitchen and bring up some of our tuna," I said urgently. "Maybe if we give 'em some scraps they'll leave us alone."

He shrugged, raced down to the kitchen, and came up with a couple of kegs of tuna, one under each arm. We waited until two of the whales were so close we could have reached out and touched them, then threw the tuna into their gaping mouths.

Then we stood back to see if we had guessed right—and the strangest thing happened. Their eyes went wide and began watering, one of them started coughing and heaving, and the other just rolled right on its back, belly-up, which certainly agreed with my own assessment of the tuna in the first place.

The other whales took one look at their companions, then left as soon as Ishmael got some more tuna and began throwing it at them.

Not too much happened after that, at least so far as whales and savages were concerned. Ishmael told me that the Slavs were getting ready to take over the ship if we didn't start feeding them meat, but I figured that we were only a few days out of port and there wasn't much sense stopping to find a source of meat this close to the end of our little voyage.

Then, when we were just one day out of Cape Horn, the belly dancer approached me and asked if, in my dual capacity as captain of *The Dying Quail* and a man of the cloth, I could perform marriages onboard the ship.

There was a little confusion just then, since I began explaining that I could consummate marriages with the best of them, but we finally got things straightened out, and that evening after dinner I pronounced her and the actor man and wife, the sentences to run concurrently.

"That was very well done, sir," said Luthor, stopping by my table after the ceremony.

"Oh, indeed it was, sir," agreed Ishmael, joining him.

"Well, thank you very much, brothers," I said. "Always happy to oblige young love in bloom."

"We were rather hoping you'd feel that way about it, sir," said Luthor.

"I'm not sure I follow you," I said.

"You may not have noticed it, sir," said Ishmael, "but young love has been blooming all over the whole ruddy boat."

"Another marriage?" I said. "Bring 'em up here in front of me and I'll have 'em hitched in no time."

"Well, this one is a bit irregular," said Ishmael, leaning over and whispering in my ear.

I agreed as how it was a mite out of the ordinary, but once we got to haggling in earnest I found that fifty pounds was more than enough to assuage my conscience and eliminate any hint of irregularity, and an hour after the first ceremony, I married the three German girls to Ishmael, Luthor, and three of their shipmates.

The man on watch called out that Cape Horn was within sight, and yet another couple decided that if they were ever going to get married, they would probably find less social opposition here than elsewhere. Fifty more pounds changed hands, and a few moments later I joined Kim Li Sang, the Korean dermatologist, to Eduardo Duarte, the Paraguayan writer.

I made sure that there were no more weddings in the near offing, then called Ishmael and Luthor up from their rather crowded bridal bower. Luthor had a black eye, and Ishmael was missing a tooth.

"What the hell happened?" I asked.

"We had our first lovers' tiff," said Ishmael, spitting a little blood over the railing.

"You ought to see the other six!" added Luthor.

"Later, perhaps," I said. "I've called you here for something a little more important."

"And what might that be, sir?" asked Luthor.

"Do the Slavs still want to take over the ship?"

"Indeed they do, sir," said Ishmael.

"Good," I said. "Why don't you give me just enough time to move my gear out of Captain Roberts's quarters, and then tell them the ship is all theirs."

When the ship docked the next morning, there was a welcoming committee waiting for us, led by Captain Roberts himself. Evidently he had been fished out of the ocean by a passing cargo ship, which, not bothering to explore the Congo River and its environs, had beaten us to the Cape by almost a full day.

The Slavs, who by this time had moved lock, stock, and barrel into the captain's quarters, were jailed as mutineers pending the outcome of an admiralty inquiry, while Ishmael Bledsoe and

Luthor Christian were given citations of commendation for getting *The Dying Quail* into port only a day late, and were exonerated of all wrongdoing not directly connected with their wedding. The last I saw of them, they were sneaking off to parts unknown with the rest of their newly-made little family just as a Slavic translator arrived on the scene.

As for me, I had one hundred crisp British pounds in my pocket, and having had my fill of the sea, I set off once again in search of the fortune that would finally result in the building of the Tabernacle of Saint Luke.

8. AN AFFAIR OF THE HEART

Cape Town didn't appear all that promising a place for the ex-captain of *The Dying Quail* to settle down, especially once Captain Roberts figured out why he'd been tossed overboard and started looking for me with a gun, so I took my leave one fine morning at about two o'clock and headed on up the eastern coastline. My money held out just fine until I got to Durban, which had a mule track, horses being too expensive for that part of the country. I picked out a likely-looking one named Saint Andrew, placed my money down. and watched him go into the final turn leading by two lengths when a pride of lions raced out of the veldt and attacked the field.

The jockeys, most of whom were faster than their mounts anyway, jumped off and raced to safety, but none of the mules made it as far as the homestretch. The track, claiming that this was an act of God, refused to refund the bets, even though I, representing God, pointed out that what it mostly was was an act of lions. I could see we were likely to be arguing all day without solving anything, so I took the rest of my money and tried to put it all on a large black-maned lion who was just finishing off Saint Andrew. The track officials explained that it was against policy to make book on lions, and besides, they wouldn't give me more than three-to-five on the black-maned one.

We did some real quick haggling amongst ourselves and finally they laid nine-to-ten against my lion, with no place or show betting. As soon as I put up my money the lion got up, yawned, stretched, and ambled back into the bush.

"Off the course! Foul!" cried the steward. "Disqualified and placed last."

"How come you didn't disqualify him for eating Saint Andrew?" I demanded.

"My dear sir," said the steward in a patronizing voice, "he ran straight and true after Saint Andrew."

"I'm afraid I don't follow you, brother," I said.

"There is nothing in the rules about one participant eating another," he continued. "But it clearly states that leaving the course is a foul."

"Am I to understand, brother," I said, "that you have no intention of refunding either of my bets?"

He nodded.

"Who's in charge here?" I demanded. "I want to see the owner."

"The owner is Mrs. Emily Perrison," said the steward, "but you won't find her here. She detests gambling."

"Then why the hell does she own a racetrack?" I asked.

"For the same reason she owns almost everything else in this town: Her husband died and left it to her."

"A widow, you say. Is she young?"

"Old enough to be your mother," replied the steward. "And crazy as all get-out. Gives away most of her money to religious missions up north of here."

"Where in particular?" I asked.

"Like I told you: up north."

"The whole world's up north," I pointed out.

"I don't know: Ethiopia, Chad, the Sudan. Somewhere up there."

"How would I find this Mrs. Perrison?" I asked.

"I can't give out her address," he said, "but if you'll just walk north and east you can't miss it."

I left both the racetrack and my hundred pounds behind me without a second thought. I had a few shillings left in my pocket, and I spent them on a shave and a little hair grease, after which I started walking to the northeast. The steward hadn't been kidding about not being able to miss my destination, because I soon passed, in rapid succession, Perrison's Dry Goods, Perrison's General Store, Perrison's Slaughterhouse and Restaurant, and the *Perrison Daily Press*. When I finally reached the long roadway leading to the Perrison homestead it was twilight, and it was dark by the time I walked up to the huge old wooden farmhouse.

I spent a couple of minutes smoothing down my hair, brushing the dust off my clothes, and making sure the Good Book was prominently displayed, then knocked on the door. It was opened a moment later by a fat young man with a sullen face and piggy little eyes.

"What do you want?" he whined.

"Greetings," I said pleasantly. "Is Emily Perrison at home?"

"Who wants to know?" he asked, picking on a pimple.

"What do you mean, who wants to know?" I said. "*I* want to know."

"Who are you?" he asked, rubbing his stubby little nose.

"I am Doctor Lucifer Jones," I said, forcing a friendly smile.

"My mum don't need a doctor," he said sullenly.

"I'm not that kind of doctor," I said. "Why not get your mother and let her decide?"

He grunted, slammed the door in my face, and left me standing out there in the cold. A minute passed, then another, and finally the door opened again and I found myself facing Mrs. Emily Perrison.

She was the pinkest woman I ever did see. She wore her hair up in a bun, and her face and body looked like someone was trying to balance a small balloon atop a bigger one. She had blue eyes, a broad nose, and lots of shiny white teeth, and she looked like she would never walk when she could mince.

She reached out a ruffled arm and took my hand in hers.

"Doctor Jones?"

"The Right Reverend Doctor Lucifer Jones," I said, stooping over and kissing her fingers. They tasted of bread dough, and it reminded me that I hadn't eaten all day. "I'm back from your mission in Ethiopia to report on all the good work we've been doing with the money you so generously sent to us."

"But I made no contributions to Ethiopia," she said, looking puzzled.

"Well, they *told* me I was in Ethiopia, but it could have been Chad."

"I *do* make donations to a number of missions in Chad," she said.

"And right appreciative we are," I said quickly. "It would just melt your heart to see all those little heathen children coming to church and singing hymns of a Sunday morning."

Her face lit up at that, and she invited me into the living room, which had a flock of overstuffed Victorian chairs and loveseats covered by hundreds of little doilies. There were a batch of paintings on the wall, mostly of flowers and apples and stuff like that, but they didn't hold a candle to the painting of Nellie Willoughby in the altogether that hung over the bar in the New Stanley Hotel.

"By the way, who was that who met me at the door?" I asked.

"That was my son, Horace," she said apologetically.

"A right charming lad he is," I said quickly.

"Well, Doctor Jones," she said with a fluttery little sigh, "I've heard Horace called a good many things, but that's the very first time the word charming has ever been mentioned."

"All he needs is a little firm guidance from a Godfearing stepfather not unlike myself and he'll be right as rain."

"I'm glad you agree," she said.

"Agree with who and about what?" I asked.

"With me, about Horace. I've recently allowed a certain gentleman to come calling, mainly because I too feel that the boy needs a father."

That wasn't exactly the solution I had in mind, but I just smiled and allowed as to how I'd like to meet such a lucky fellow before going back into the bush for another couple of quick rounds with Satan.

She told me that I was in luck because he was coming over for dinner that very night. Then she got me some tea and started asking about the natives in Chad. I told her whatever sounded likely, embellishing a little bit here and there about their fertility rites and other such rituals, and explaining that it was due to her and her alone that these sinful goings-on had been stopped.

Suddenly she reached out, grabbed my hand, and held it against her bosom, which was considerable when at rest but was throbbing to beat the band right then.

"It must have been terribly difficult for a cultured gentleman like yourself to rub shoulders with such savages!" she said.

"Somebody had to do it," I said nobly. "And what Christian wouldn't gladly accept a little torture and some tropical diseases if it enabled him to spread the Word?" I shot her my saddest, most tragic smile. "And while I may have missed the companionship of a good Christian white woman during all them painful years, I couldn't have afforded to keep a wife or raise a family anyway, what with donating all my money to various leper colonies."

"You poor dear!" she breathed. "You're penniless?"

I nodded. "But I ain't complaining, ma'am," I said quickly. "I've got spiritual riches, and that's something I wouldn't trade with no one."

"Where did you plan to spend the night?" she asked.

"I saw a real comfortable-looking bench behind the slaughterhouse," I said. "And I'm sure in a week or two I can get used to the smell."

"I won't hear of it!" she exclaimed. "You'll stay right here in the house as our guest until you're ready to go out and do the Lord's work again."

"But ma'am," I protested. "It just ain't right. Besides, I still get nightmares from the time they strung me up and tried to make me renounce Jesus. You wouldn't want to wake up during all that screaming. I mean, I know you feel deeply obligated because I've undergone all this suffering and privation for your pet charities, but . . ."

"You're staying, and that's that!" she said firmly.

I explained that it was morally wrong but that I was too weak and exhausted to argue with her anymore, so I'd have to abide by her decision. She was just reaching out to grab my face and press it on her bosom right next to my hand, and I took a deep breath on the assumption that there wasn't a lot of extra room there for air or anything else, when we were interrupted by a brisk knocking at the front door.

She stood up, slightly flushed and looking pinker than ever, and walked to the door. A moment later she returned with a familiar figure who was dressed all in black: shirt, tie, vest, suit, socks, shoes, hat, belt, probably even underwear.

"Doctor Jones," said Emily, "I'd like to introduce you to my gentleman caller, Major Theodore Dobbins, late of His Majesty's armed forces."

I'm not sure which of us looked more surprised, but he recovered first and extended his hand.

"My dear Doctor Jones," he said. "How good it is to see you again!"

"You two know each other?" asked Emily.

"We've done a little missionary work together," I said. "In fact, I think you could fairly say that the last time we got together we prevented a few hundred poor lost souls from becoming drug addicts."

"Praise God!" she cried, looking all sort of uplifted.

"It's been a long time, Doctor Jones," said the Major, seating himself on one of the uglier chairs. "I had never expected to see you again."

"Isn't it a small world?" said Emily.

"Crowded is more the word for it," I replied.

"Well, I'll leave you two to discuss old times while I check on dinner," she said, scurrying out to the kitchen.

"What are *you* doing here?" Major Dobbins hissed as soon as she was out of earshot.

"Just spreading the word of the Lord," I replied. "And yourself?"

"You will doubtless find this difficult to comprehend," he said, "but I am here because of an earnest affair of the heart."

"Difficult ain't exactly the word I'd choose, Brother Dobbins," I said. "How much is she worth?"

"What makes you think I'd know anything about her financial status?" he said with dignity. "I assure you, my friend, that such a question has never crossed my mind."

"*That* much?" I said.

"My dear Doctor Jones," he said, sitting down opposite me, "I think it best that we lay all our cards on the table. After our unfortunate meeting with Erich Von Horst in Dar-es-Salaam, certain business interests caused me to move my base of operations to South Africa in some degree of haste."

"They issued another warrant for you?" I asked.

"Let us say that my interpretations of the finer points of the law differed in various respects from those of the authorities," he replied. "Be that as it may, I found that I had insufficient capital to continue dealing in those perishable goods that had formed the staple of my livelihood for the past decade. Indeed, all seemed hopeless until I heard of the good Mrs. Perrison from an associate, and immediately moved my base once again, this time to Durban. I will confess that she does indeed possess a certain amount of wealth, though doubtless far less than you hope or suspect. I have been courting her assiduously for the past two months, and now stand upon the brink of being able to set the time and place for our nuptials."

"It certainly beats leaving it all to Horace," I said thoughtfully.

"I knew you would appreciate my position," he said with a smile.

"I do more than appreciate it, Major," I replied. "I *envy* it."

"And so we come to the crux of the situation," he said. "Exactly how much will it take to assuage your envy?"

"I sure wouldn't want to appear greedy or nothing," I told him. "But I got a feeling that it would take more than you're willing to spend."

"Two thousand pounds," he offered.

"Come on, now, Major," I said. "I walked by all those stores on the way up here."

"They all have mortgages," he replied. "Two thousand is a generous offer, Doctor Jones."

"I never denied it," I said. "Of course, it stands to reason that if two thousand is a generous offer, ten thousand is five times as generous."

"That is simply out of the question," he said. "Let's split it right down the middle: twenty-five hundred pounds."

I shook my head. "Well, Major, it looks like we're going to be rivals for that poor lonesome widow lady's hand. May the best man win, so long as he ain't an Englishman with a price on his head."

Emily rejoined us just then to inform us that dinner was on the table, and we followed her into the dining room, which, like the living room, was furnished with a batch of ugly Victorian items, in this case a china cabinet with a matching table and four dumpy chairs. Horace was sitting on one of the chairs, picking his nose thoughtfully, and the Major and I sat down at the head and foot of the table. Emily joined us a few seconds later.

"I'm sure you gentlemen had lots to talk about," said Emily.

"More than you could imagine," I assured her.

"Have you known each other long?" she asked.

"Oh, we go way back, ma'am," I said. "Of course, Major Dobbins goes a lot farther back than I do, me being a young and vital God-fearing Christian gentleman in the very prime of life."

"My dear Doctor Jones, you must learn not to feel so self-conscious about your unworldliness and lack of experience," said the Major. "After all, immaturity is nothing to be ashamed of. You'll undoubtedly outgrow it at about the same time Horace does."

With that, Horace got up from the table and stalked out of the room.

"Have I said something to offend him?" asked the Major with a certain degree of satisfaction.

"He's a very sensitive boy," Emily replied.

"I could tell that right off the bat," I interjected.

"He's still trying to find himself," she confided.

"Has he tried looking in the kitchen?" I asked. "I mean, if I wanted to find Horace, that's the very first place I'd look for him."

"You must excuse my friend," said the Major. "I'm sure he doesn't mean to appear so boorish, but I must also point out that it is this very insensitivity that precludes his ever successfully raising a child."

"Just because you've been littering Africa with children don't give you no monopoly on fatherly wisdom," I shot back. "I could raise Horace as well as the next man, especially if the next man was you."

"I'm afraid I don't follow what all this is about," said Emily.

"Miss Emily," I said, "I got to declare myself here and now. I've lost my heart to the radiance of your beauty, and want nothing more than to be a husband to you and a good father to Horace, teaching him the manly art of self-defense and taking him to rugby games of a Sunday afternoon."

"This is so sudden!" she said, blushing. "But what about the Major?"

"He can go out and preach the Word amongst the heathen like I been doing," I said. "It might do him a world of good."

"I'll need time to think about this," said Emily.

"My dear, I urge you not to listen to him," said the Major. "If nothing else, think of Horace. Doctor Jones is probably even now wanted in some municipality or another for pederasty."

"That's a lie!" I shouted. "I ain't never pretended to be a foot doctor in my life! Miss Emily, I put it to you: The only person at this table who has ever been arrested is the Major."

"Is that true, Theodore?" she asked.

"It was a very trivial matter, my dear," he said.

"That's what all them naked ladies said too."

Emily Perrison gasped and covered her face with her hands.

"By gad, sir, I will not be subjected to any further vilifications!" roared the Major. "Honor demands satisfaction!"

That brought back memories of a lively young girl I used to know back in the States named Honor Weinburger, but before I could share this drollery with them the Major was on his feet, pacing back and forth and thumping his fist into his palm.

"We'll meet at dawn!" he said at last. "Jones, choose your weapon!"

"How about silence at five hundred paces?" I suggested when I saw he was serious. "You could start now."

"Pistols!" said the Major. "Pistols at the count of ten."

"This is silly, Major," I said. "I ain't never fired a pistol in my life, and you ain't never made close friends with anyone who could count all the way up to ten."

"Humbug!" cried the Major. "You're trying to make a farce out of this just to hide your cowardice!"

"And you're trying to make a duel out of it because you know you ain't got a chance next to a handsome young buck like me," I said. "Begging your pardon for being so immodest and truthful, ma'am."

"May I say something?" asked Emily, who had been looking more and more upset.

"I'm afraid not, my dear," said the Major. "This is an *affaire d'honneur* now."

"But what if I don't want to marry the winner?" she said.

"That's absolutely unheard of!" snapped Major Dobbins.

"I got to agree with the Major," I said. "If I actually get around to risking my life for your hand, I'd just naturally expect the rest of you to come with it."

"It's *my* hand," she pointed out.

"But it's *our* duel," replied the Major. "Women simply don't understand these things."

"Now just a minute!" said Emily hotly.

"Madame, I love you with a mad undying passion that admits of no doubt or weakness, " said the Major, placing a hand to his heart. "And I cannot in good conscience allow this scoundrel to turn your head and destroy your chance for happiness, to say nothing of the detrimental influence he would have on young Horace, of whom I could not be more fond if he were my own son."

I must confess that I shared his sentiments about Horace, and would have been hard pressed to name a situation that could have made me any fonder of him either, especially if he were my own son.

Well, Miss Emily kind of softened when she heard the Major's declaration of love and high purpose, which forced me to make a similar one, and she finally agreed as to how sometimes affairs of honor were kind of honorable.

"But I do have one small request, Theodore," she said.

"Whatever you wish, my dear," he replied smoothly.

"Could you fight your duel at noon instead of sunrise?"

"Certainly," he said. "But why?"

"I thought we might hold it at the racetrack and charge a little something extra for admission. The missions in Chad and the

Sudan could surely use the money, and somehow all this won't seem so futile if it serves a good purpose."

"Ah, what a rare treasure one of us is going to be marrying, eh?" smiled the Major.

"True," I agreed. "And what a lovely woman comes with it."

The Major harrumphed a couple of times and then got to his feet. "Excuse me, one and all, but I think I'd best be returning to my apartments," he announced.

"But it's only eight o'clock," protested Emily in hurt tones.

"True," he acknowledged. "But I plan to have a hard day of butchery and bloodletting tomorrow, and I do that sort of thing best after a good night's sleep. Why not come along with me, Doctor Jones? We can toast one another's good if brief health a few times, and you won't be besmirching our dearly beloved lady's reputation by spending the night here without a chaperone."

"I'd like to oblige you, Major," I said, "but someone ought to stay here to protect our fragile flower from jungle beasts and other night critters. Don't feel badly about not thinking of it yourself, though; it's the kind of thought that would only occur to a decent and dedicated young missionary."

He glared at me for a couple of minutes, then turned on his heel and left. By the time Emily and I got back to the dining room we found Horace sitting at the table, working on his fourth piece of pie.

"You gonna fight for my mum?" he asked between mouthfuls.

"It sure appears that that's the course the Lord has in mind for me," I said. "Will you be rooting for me, Horace?"

"Don't know," he said, downing a quart of milk in a single swallow. "Have to see the morning line first."

"Horace!" said Emily.

"Just boyish enthusiasm," I said, tousling his hair and dislodging a couple of flies in the process. "He'll outgrow it if he lives long enough."

We went out to the parlor and had a sip or two of brandy, and then I was shown to my room. It seemed that my head had hardly hit the pillow before Horace was shaking me and telling me to hurry up or else I'd be late for the duel.

"Well, they can't start without me," I muttered, sitting up on the bed.

"I laid twenty shillings on the Major at one-to-two," said Horace, "and I don't win if you forfeit."

I thanked the little ghoul for his concern, dressed as quickly as I could, and walked down to the kitchen, where Emily was frying up some eggs.

"No time for eating, Mum!" cried Horace, grabbing my arm and dragging me to the door. "We're late!"

"But . . ." said Emily.

"We're *late!*" repeated Horace, almost in a panic.

She sighed, shrugged, and followed us out to a carriage, which Horace had already attached to a couple of horses. We flew down the streets of Durban as if we were being pulled by Exterminator and Old Rosebud, and within twenty minutes or so we pulled up at the racetrack. Major Dobbins was waiting for us at the finish line with the track steward.

"My dear Doctor Jones," he said, extending his hand as we approached him. "I trust you slept well. You know, I have been giving the matter considerable thought, and have concluded that this is really a rather barbaric way of settling our little dispute."

"My own sentiments exactly," I said.

"Would you consider some other means of so doing?" he asked.

"Such as?"

"We could cut a deck of cards," he said, producing just such a deck.

"Now just a minute!" said Emily. "I'm not one to encourage bloodshed, Lord knows, but while I can see certain justifications for an affair of honor, cutting cards for my hand just doesn't qualify as such."

"Besides," said the steward, "we have charged all thousand spectators an extra shilling per head. We're likely to have a riot if you call the thing off."

"Well, my friend," said the Major, "it would seem that we have no choice." He gestured to a track official, who walked up with a mahogany box containing two pistols.

I was offered first choice, and since they looked alike to me I just grabbed the one that was closer. Evidently I did it with such skill and swiftness that the crowd thought I knew what I was doing, because a little murmur of approval spread through them. The Major took the other one and we stood back-to-back at the finish line.

"At my signal," said the steward, "you will each take ten paces, turn, and fire. Any fouls and/or disqualifications will be at the discretion of the track's governing board. Are you ready?"

"Yes," said the Major.

"I suppose so," I said.

"Good," said the steward. "Proceed."

The Major must have taken quicker steps than me, because I heard two shots before I got to my tenth step.

"False start!" cried the steward.

"Now what?" I asked, turning around.

"You do it again until you get it right," said the steward.

So we did it again, and this time we turned and faced each other at the same instant. I heard a lot of shots coming from the Major's direction, and I just closed my eyes, pointed the gun toward him, and kept firing until I was out of bullets.

"Halt!" cried the steward.

"What now?" demanded the Major.

"You wounded nine spectators and killed a mule," said the steward disgustedly. "Are you sure you want to continue with this?"

"Absolutely," said the Major.

"All right, then," said the steward as we re-loaded our weapons. "This time get back to back and only go five paces. Maybe *that* will help."

Well, to make a long story short, we each fired off six more bullets, and nothing much happened except that we took the head off a Guinea hen that had wandered onto the track by mistake. The crowd started getting ugly then, and one of them threw a rock that grazed the Major's skull.

"Foul!" he cried, and fell to the dirt track.

"How is he?" I asked, moseying over.

"'Tis a far far better thing I do than I have ever done," said the Major.

"Oh, get up!" snapped the steward. "I've seen fly bites draw more blood than that!"

The Major got uneasily to his feet and waved a victory sign to the crowd, which booed in return.

"May I make a suggestion?" said the steward.

"Shoot," I said, and the Major hit the ground again. "What's the matter now?" I asked, helping him to his feet.

"You might select your words a little more carefully," he said sternly.

"My suggestion?" said the steward impatiently.

"Go ahead," I said.

"Since you two are not the most skillful marksmen I have ever seen, I suggest that we might bring this unhappy affair of honor to a conclusion a mite quicker if you switched to swords."

"A capital suggestion!" cried the Major enthusiastically.

A moment later a couple of military sabers were brought out. They had to show me how to hold mine, but the Major grabbed his like it was an old friend and started swishing it through the air as if he was slicing mosquitoes in half.

"Are you ready?" asked the steward.

"Not by a long shot," I said, still trying out how to hold it without sticking my thumb over the bell.

"Too damned bad," said the steward. "Proceed."

The Major gave me a great big grin and a great big salute with his sword, and I figured that me and the Lord would be hobnobbing in person in just a couple more seconds. Then he lunged forward at me, and I heard something that sounded like a gunshot, only louder.

"Owww!" he screamed, and I noticed that he was standing still as a statue, which was kind of difficult since he was all stretched out, one leg dragging behind him and one arm extended toward me.

"What happened?" I asked him, putting my sword down and staring at him with my hands on my hips.

"I must have thrown my back out!" he grated. "I can't move!"

Well, me and the steward called time out and tried to straighten the Major up, but he sure enough wasn't kidding about being stuck in that position. After about ten minutes we gave up and I walked over to Emily Perrison.

"Miss Emily," I said, "I just don't think I'd feel right about killing the Major under these conditions, him being helpless and all—and especially not with so many witnesses."

"I understand," she said, patting my hand. "It's your Christian goodness rising to the fore."

"I'm glad nobody got killed," I said.

"So am I," she smiled.

"I'm not," said Horace sullenly.

"Well, then," I said, "if you'll just name the happy date, Miss Emily, I'll announce our nuptials to all and sundry."

"I've been giving the matter some serious thought during these past few minutes, Lucifer," she said slowly, "and I have decided to give myself in marriage to Major Dobbins."

"But why?" I said. "I mean, I could go over and slice him up a little if that's all that stands in the way of our getting hitched."

"It's more than that, Lucifer," she said. "You're so good and pure and true, such a Christian gentleman, that you'd never be happy tied down to a family in a dull little city like Durban when you could be off converting cannibals and lepers and the like. Whereas Major Dobbins, on the other hand, has a certain weakness of the spirit that makes his salvation a real challenge to me."

"But Miss Emily, *I* can be just as weak as *he* can!" I protested.

"No, I won't hear of it," she said firmly. "You're too good for me, Lucifer. It's the Major who wanted my money, while you only wanted to serve our God."

"Suppose I wanted your money, too," I said. "Would that make a difference to you?"

"Don't be silly!" she laughed. "You're too fine and pure to think such sordid thoughts."

"I am?" I asked unhappily.

"Absolutely. Now you and the Major will each get what you want, and I'll have made both of you happy."

"But . . ."

"Onward Christian Soldier!" she cried with a wild evangelical gleam in her eye.

I took one last look at Horace and decided that staying single might not be the worst of all possible fates, so I took my leave of Durban while they were still trying to decide whether to take the Major to a doctor or coat him over with paint and use him as a lawn statue.

I camped north of town that night and had a little heart-to-heart with my Silent Partner, who pointed out that He had littered South Africa with diamonds and other baubles and that, as long as I was here anyway, this might not be a bad time to look for them.

It sounded good to me, and I headed inland in search of my fortune, determined to keep no diamonds under eighteen carats.

9. THE LOST RACE

You know, diamonds are a lot harder to find than you might think. I must have spent the better part of two weeks looking in caves and gorges and riverbeds and valleys and abandoned rock quarries without finding a single one. I even checked out a couple of exotic-looking orchards, just in case I was dead wrong about where diamonds came from, but I finally had to admit that there was more to the diamond-prospecting business than met the eye.

Since I was fresh out of funds (actually, there's wasn't nothing *fresh* about it—I'd been out of funds for quite a long time), I took a job dealing faro when I hit Germiston, a quaint little village a couple of miles east of Johannesburg. I gave it up after a couple of days, though, after I earned enough money to buy a second-hand Chautauqua tent.

I supplemented my meager preaching income by hosting a few friendly games of bingo until I realized that the bingo cards were costing me more than I was winning from the natives, since there wasn't much of a market for boers' teeth and such other trinkets as they used for legal tender, and finally I made up my mind to light out for Nairobi the next day to see if I couldn't scare up a little more money in British East Africa than I was finding in the Down Under side of the continent.

I told my helpers to show up at noon for their severance pay, but then I got to thinking about the story of Job and decided that a little hardship and disappointment was probably just the kind of strengthening and hardening their spirits needed, so I turned in early and made up my mind to leave town a bit before daybreak. I was snoring away in my hotel room, minding my own business and not bothering no one, when I was awakened by the sound of a door opening.

I sat up, rubbed my eyes, and saw as pretty a little lady as I had ever experienced standing in my doorway. She was dressed all in blue silks and veils that didn't hide half as much as she thought they did, and she had the strangest headdress topping her yellow hair.

"Have you got it?" she whispered, walking into the room and closing the door behind her.

"Ma'am," I said with a smile, "I've got *it*, and to spare. To what do I owe the distinct pleasure of this here nocturnal visitation?"

"The Malaloki armband," she said. "Where is it?"

"Probably in Malaloki, wherever that may be," I answered. "However, you're welcome to search every inch of me, which I'm sure you'll agree is a pretty generous offer to make to a total stranger."

"But you *must* have it!" she hissed.

"I don't know what you're talking about," I answered.

"You *are* Lucifer Jones, are you not?"

"The Right Reverend Lucifer Jones at your service," I said. "You *sure* you don't want to search me for this here armband?"

"This is not a matter for levity," she said sternly.

"Neither is breaking and entering," I pointed out. "Though," I added, "the Lord does teach us to forgive our brother's trespasses. Of course, He don't say much about our sister's trespasses, but I'm sure you and me can work something out if we just put our heads together."

"I will ask you one more time: Where is it?"

"I don't know," I said with a shrug. "On the other hand, I sure am glad that you've asked me for the last time. What would you like to talk about now?"

She looked at me, frowned, and opened the door, and before I knew it two big white guys dressed in leopardskin robes had burst into the room and were threatening me with spears. They both had on the same kind of headdresses as the girl, kind of feathery with a couple of little jewels right at the front hanging down over their foreheads, but somehow the headdresses didn't look as good on them, or maybe it was just that they kept jabbing me in the short ribs with the points of their weapons.

"I must have that armband, Mister Jones," said the girl.

"*Doctor* Jones," I corrected her, sucking in my stomach as far as I could as the spears kept pressing against it.

"Make no mistake about it, Doctor Jones," she said. "Two men have already died this evening."

"I hope it wasn't nothin' catching," I said with as much compassion as I could muster, which truth to tell wasn't near as much as I might have had under other circumstances.

"They died because of the Malaloki armband," she said meaningfully.

"What is it—some kind of wrestling hold?" I asked.

"An ancient and sacred ornament of the Malaloki, which may be worn only by one of our gods."

"Well, I hate to disappoint a lovable little lady like yourself," I said, "but despite my handsome and clean-cut good looks, I ain't no god."

"The Malaloki armband was stolen two moons past by a disloyal subject," she continued impassively. "We traced it to Germiston, and here we lost it—until tonight. The man who had stolen it had traded it for food and other worldly goods, the storekeeper had sold it to a Boer, the Boer had given it to a black house servant, and the servant lost it to you in a game of chance. You have it, and now you must give it to us or your life shall be forfeit."

"But I ain't seen any armbands!" I said as they began prodding me a little harder with their spear tips. "Not gold nor silver nor brass nor any kind."

"*Wait!*" she commanded, holding her hand imperiously above her head, and suddenly the two guys with the weapons backed off a bit. "Possibly you do not as yet know the shape and texture of that about which I speak. The Malaloki armband has no commercial value, but is made of shells joined together in a mystic design of overwhelming power and import."

"Well, why didn't you say so in the first place?" I said. "I took in what I thought was a little ankle bracelet made of strung-together shells."

"The *armband!*" she exclaimed, finally showing some emotion, even if not the kind I would have preferred to see from a blonde in a see-through blue wraparound.

"I think it's worthless, you think it's priceless," I said. "How's about we split the difference and I trade it to you for a couple of them jewels off your headdresses, unless they got some special religious significance too?"

"Doctor Jones," she said, "we will trade you your life for the armband. That should constitute a considerable profit for you."

"Considering the alternative, I suppose I could do a mite worse," I admitted begrudgingly.

"Where is it?"

"I've got a whole bag of junk—begging your pardon—over at my tent. Wait'll I get my clothes on, and I'll take you there."

Which I did, though we must have made a funny-looking sight stalking through the narrow streets of Germiston at three in the morning. I couldn't see much sense returning to the hotel just to wake the desk clerk, so I slipped a deck of cards into my pocket and made up my mind to head right off for Nairobi once our business was done.

When we got to the tent it turned out that none of us had any matches, so I just started walking around, kind of feeling blindly for the bag. After a couple of minutes I stepped on something that made a pretty loud crunching sound, and I knew that I had found the trinket.

The girl ran over and started pulling stuff out of the bag, and a couple of seconds later she gave out a shriek that would have woke such dead as weren't otherwise occupied at the time.

"What seems to be the problem, ma'am?" I asked out of an innate sense of courtesy.

"It's broken!" she cried, holding up a bunch of busted shells that were hanging together by a few torn threads.

"That's a shame," I said sympathetically. "Maybe you could hunt up some clams or oysters or something and stitch up a replacement."

"You do not understand what this means," she wept.

"Maybe even lobster shells," I added thoughtfully. "There's a pretty good seafood shop over in Johannesburg, and . . ."

"Silence!" roared one of the two men, pointing his spear at me.

I didn't see much sense in making helpful suggestions if that was the way they had been taught to respond to an act of Christian goodwill, so I just stood there while the three of them went into a little pow-wow. Finally they broke it up and the girl walked over to me.

"You will come with us," she announced.

"I really had other plans," I said, and started telling her about how I aimed to build the Tabernacle of Saint Luke. I got about three sentences into my story when one of the men started jabbing me with his spear again.

"You will come with us," she repeated. "You will speak to our gods and tell them how the armband came to be broken, and possibly they will spare our lives."

I took another close look at all their various jewels, which sure seemed pretty common and unimportant to them, and made up my mind on the spot. "I'll be happy to come along with you," I said with a great big smile. "You may not know it, but speaking to gods is one of the very best things I do, me being a man of the cloth and all."

We stepped out of the tent and began walking to the north. After we had gotten a couple of miles out of town, the girl turned to me again.

"I hope you understand, Doctor Jones," she said, "that any attempt to escape while we make our way to Malaloki will be dealt with severely."

"I give you my word as a Christian and a gentleman that such a thought ain't never crossed my mind," I said truthfully, naturally assuming that such a verbal contract expired once we got to wherever they kept their jewels.

Well, we walked and we walked and then we walked some more. I kept assuming that Cairo or Marrakech would pop into view any second, but she assured me that we were still in South Africa, and that we weren't heading no farther than Nyasaland, which I hadn't never heard of before, and which I now began picturing as a great huge field of grass with a bunch of baby nyasas hopping around on it.

During our trek I learned that her name was Melora, and that she had learned her English from some missionaries, which was kind of surprising because it seemed like everyone I had met in Africa had learned their English from missionaries and yet I was the only bonafide missionary that I knew of wandering around in the bush. She surprised me still further by saying that her native tongue wasn't French or German or Portuguese or anything like that, but was the Malaloki dialect, which was the first time I learned that they invented languages as well as armbands.

We were about ten days into our little journey when we crossed into Nyasaland. The landscape started changing, and pretty soon the bushland turned into a kind of gently rolling forest filled with gently rolling rhinos and leopards and other fearsome beasts that looked like they wanted nothing more than a little snack made of Christian missionary and maybe a little bit of blonde Malaloki for dessert, but our two big spearmen managed to bluff all the animals away, which was undoubtedly for the best since I couldn't see how they could reload a spear if their first fling missed, and we passed through the forest unscathed except for tick bites and mosquito bites and fly bites and being bothered by some rude maribou storks that kept flying overhead right after they'd had lunch, and finally we came to a great big volcanic crater stuck right in the middle of a long plateau.

I figured that we were going to hike around it, but Melora walked straight ahead and started following a narrow little path up the side of it. I grabbed hold of her arm and explained that while the top of the crater was undoubtedly a good sight closer to God and Heaven, she didn't have to do this on my account, as I was perfectly content to worship Him from afar, or at least ground level, for a few more years, and besides the path disappeared a couple of hundred yards ahead of us.

For a woman with a short little nose, she sure made a production of looking down it at me. Finally she yanked her arm loose and started climbing again. I called ahead to her that I was going to start back down to the base of the volcano and would meet her on the other side, but no sooner were the words out of my mouth than the two big guys started jabbing me with their spears again, so I didn't have no choice but to follow her.

I did so for maybe a hundred yards when suddenly she just upped and vanished. I mean, one second I was following that beautiful round bottom up the path, which in truth was all that kept me going, and the next second she was gone, beautiful bottom and all. I stopped, scratched my head, and looked around, but couldn't see hide nor hair of her, which was a considerable amount of hide and hair to vanish from the earth all at once. Then I felt a hand on my arm, and I was dragged off the path into a narrow little tunnel.

"Where are we?" I whispered.

"Just follow me," said Melora.

"Follow you?" I repeated. "I can't even *see* you."

"Grab my hand," she said.

I reached out for it.

"*That*, Doctor Jones, is *not* my hand."

I apologized, and after a little more groping around I finally got ahold of what I was supposed to get ahold of, and pretty soon we were wending our way through this damp, winding tunnel. After about ten minutes of walking into walls and into Melora, who may have been softer than the walls but wasn't a whole lot friendlier or more understanding, we emerged onto a large ledge overlooking a village on the grassy floor of the dead volcano.

"Malaloki?" I asked.

She nodded.

A little river wended its way amongst the thatched huts, then went out through a hole it had carved out of one of the walls. This crater didn't hold a candle to some of the larger ones I was aware of, like for instance the Ngorongoro Crater in Tanganyika, but on the other hand the Ngorongoro Crater wasn't awash in jewels and blonde women, so I didn't feel no great disappointment with my current surroundings.

Melora waited until the two big guys had joined us, then led the way down another winding trail to the base of the wall.

A bunch of white women wearing even less than Melora raced up and jabbered at her in some foreign tongue. She talked right back at them, just as quick and incomprehensible, and took me by the hand and led me through the village until we came to the biggest hut, which was located smack-dab in the center. Then she bowed and backed away.

In front of the hut were two grass hammocks, and in each hammock was a grubby-looking white man with a bushy beard. One of them must have been close to seven feet tall, and the other couldn't have been more than an inch or two over five feet. Both of them were wearing khaki pants that had been cut off above the knees, and they each had a batch of necklaces made out of emeralds and sapphires and rubies and other colorful baubles.

"Well, look what we got here, brother," said the big one.

"Sure as hell don't look like no Malaloki I ever seen," said the little one.

"What's your name, stranger?" asked the big one.

"The Honorable Right Reverend Doctor Lucifer Jones at your service," I said, stooping over in a courtly bow. "Begging your pardon, but you gents sure don't sound like Malalokis from what little I've heard you speak."

"Neither do you," said the little one.

"No reason why I should," I said. "I'm an American."

"So are we," said the big one.

"Of course," added the little one, "we're also gods, but around these here parts the two ain't necessarily incompatible."

"In fact," continued the big one, "along with being gods and Americans, we're also brothers. I'm Frothingham Schmidt and he's Oglethorpe Schmidt, but them who would consider themselves our friends, or at least express an interest in ever seeing another sunrise, call us Long Schmidt and Short Schmidt."

"I'm Short Schmidt," said the little one.

"Well, I'm mighty glad to find a couple of countrymen here," I said. "You wouldn't happen to have a little something for a thirsty traveler, with maybe just enough alcohol to whip the tar out of the germs?"

"First things first," said Long Schmidt. "We ain't set foot outside our little kingdom in six years, and we got some important questions to ask about the rest of the world."

"And well you should," I said. "You'll be pleased and happy to know that we won the War to End All Wars."

"Who gives a damn about that?" said Short Schmidt. "We're Pittsburgh boys, Pittsburgh born and bred. Where did the Pirates finish last year?"

"Third or fourth, as I recollect," I answered.

"*Damn* that John McGraw!" said Long Schmidt. "Tell me, Doctor Jones—who won the Kentucky Derby of 1917?"

"Seems to me that it was Omar Khayyam," I said.

"Yahoo!" cried Short Schmidt, tossing a necklace into the air. "If we ever get back to Casey's Bar, old Flathead Mahoney is gonna owe me a double sawbuck!"

"We didn't mean to forget our manners, Doctor Jones," said Long Schmidt. "It's just that certain things are very important to us. Now we'll join you in that drink." He clapped his hands twice, and a couple of ripe young maidens brought us a round of fruit drinks, with just a little something extra added.

"So, Doctor Jones," said Short Schmidt when we had all had a couple of long swallows, "what brings you to the kingdom of the Malaloki?"

"Friendship, curiosity, an adventurous spirit, and mostly a woman named Melora," I said.

"Ah, yes, Melora," said Short Schmidt. "Lovely girl."

"Our wife," added Long Schmidt.

"One of 'em, anyway," said Short Schmidt. "Truth to tell, Jones, the blasted village is damned near overflowing with goddesses-by-marriage."

"Easy now, brother," said Long Schmidt. "Doctor Jones is a man of the cloth. Perhaps he disapproves."

"No such a thing," I assured them. "Solomon had a pile of wives, and the Good Book never said a word against him."

"Doctor Jones," said Short Schmidt with a smile, "you got the makings of a right friendly neighbor."

"Thank you kindly," I said. "You fellers mind if I ask you a couple of questions?"

"Go right ahead," said Short Schmidt.

"Who are the Malaloki, and how'd you ever get to be gods here?"

"Well, that's kind of a long story, Doctor Jones," said Long Schmidt. "Me and Short came over to Africa seven years ago to scare us up some diamonds. Didn't seem that hard when we planned it, but I'll be damned if we could find a single one."

"Diamond mines is well hid in these parts," I agreed.

"*Mines?*" exclaimed Short Schmidt. "Son of a bitch! We thunk they grew inside oysters!"

"That's pearls," I said. "Did you find any of them, at least?"

"Never even found an oyster," said Short Schmidt. "Came near to getting et by crocodiles a couple of times."

"Oh," I said. "Well, if you ever go oyster hunting again, I think you'll have a little more luck in the ocean than in the rivers."

"We ain't likely to ever see a ocean again," said Long Schmidt mournfully. "Let me get back to the main thrust of our tragic story, Doctor Jones, so you'll know why we're so happy to see you."

"Be my guest," I said, taking another drink that one of the local maidens offered me.

"Like Short told you, we came here to seek fame and fortune, mostly the latter. Matter of fact, we had a little more fame with the local constabularies than we could handle, which is how we came to take our leave of the civilized portions of Africa and head inland."

"We set up shop as traders," added Short Schmidt. "We'd make a round of the Zulus, swapping brass cartridges for goats. Then we'd trade the goats for salt, trade the salt for cattle, and sell the cattle at market. It was a tidy little business."

"So what happened?" I asked.

"Well, we had a little difference of opinion with a tribe called the Shona about whether having a couple of friendly drinks and smokes together constitutes a bonafide proposition of marriage, and we had to take our leave of them a little more quickly than we would have liked."

"Perfectly understandable," I said.

"My thoughts precisely," said Long Schmidt. "I just wish the Shona could have seen it that way. Anyway, we took off in the middle of the night, and since our bushcraft ain't exactly up to snuff, especially by Shona standards, we kept on running for two days and two nights, just to make sure that we weren't being followed too closely."

"And on the third morning," continued Short Schmidt, "we ran up against this here crater. We were both feeling kind of tired and out of sorts, what with having been running for our lives all that time, so we thought we'd climb up the wall of the crater a way and take a little rest once we were out of sight. Well, we stumbled onto some tunnel or other, and an hour later here we were, surrounded by the lost tribe of the Malaloki."

"Of course, they ain't so lost as they was," added Long Schmidt, "with both of us and now you stumbling across them, but they're lost enough. I don't think we'll ever get out of here."

"Make up your mind," I said. "Are you gods or are you prisoners?"

"Well, truth to tell," said Short Schmidt, "there seems to be a fine and highly technical legal line between the two. Seems that their legends told of a couple of gods who would come here disguised as white men."

"Well, you got no problem that I can see," I said.

"Hah!" snorted Long Schmidt.

"The problem," said Short Schmidt, "is that two *other* white guys wandered in here about fifty years ago, and after they'd got all the ladies pregnant and picked up the choicer gemstones, they just up and left."

"So the Malaloki have decided that as long as we stay here we must be gods, and we can do damned near anything we want," continued Long Schmidt. "But the second we leave, we've proved that we're just men after all, and they've got about twenty beefy young men on the other side of that crater wall waiting to make pincushions out of us."

"I can see where that might get to be a nuisance," I agreed.

"That's why we sent Melora after you," said Short Schmidt.

"By the way," I said, "I'm supposed to tell you that Melora didn't break the sacred armband. I kind of stomped on it accidentally."

"'Tain't noways sacred anyhow," said Short Schmidt. "We knew that one of the young bucks was going to Germiston for some seeds to plant, so we snuck it into his pouch and told Melora that he'd went and swiped a sacred object."

"How come?" I asked.

"Melora ain't exactly the most humorous critter we've ever run into," said Long Schmidt. "We figured she'd move heaven and earth to get that armband back, and we were kind of hoping that she'd wipe out enough locals so that someone would follow her back here, like maybe an army or something big like that."

"So while we're delighted to see a fellow countryman, and especially one who knows how the Pirates are doing these days," said Short Schmidt, "I'd have to say that on the whole you represent a considerable disappointment to us, meaning no offense."

"None taken," I said. "Who *are* the Malaloki, anyway?"

"As near as we can figure it," said Long Schmidt, "they're the descendants of some Roman outpost. Probably been living in the crater some fifteen hundred years or so. A few of 'em leave every now and then to buy things we can get down here and to learn a little English, but they always come back. For a while there me and Short really talked up the outside world in the hope that one by one they'd all go out and make their way and leave us alone here with the jewels, but so far it ain't happened."

"So here we are," concluded Short Schmidt, "gods of the Malaloki, with the power of life and death over our subjects and every whim catered to—so long as we don't walk more than six hundred yards from where we are now. We may never see the Pirates again!"

"Power of life and death, you say?" I asked.

"We're gods, ain't we?"

"Why not kill 'em off and just walk out free as birds?" I suggested.

"We've thunk it over long and hard," admitted Short Schmidt. "But while we don't back off none at a little serious swindling and cardsharking, murdering a whole lost tribe would probably put us off our feed."

"Of course, we may eventually get around to killing off all the menfolk," added Long Schmidt. "I don't like the way they look at us whenever we get married, which is pretty damned often now that I come to think of it."

"Well, now, brothers," I said, "you sound right happy and fulfilled as things stand. What in the world would you do if you ever got out of here?"

"Run like hell," said Short Schmidt devoutly.

"I mean after that," I said.

"See if we couldn't land us a grubstake and marry us a couple of good women and settle down, making sure to buy lifetime season tickets to the Pirates. Is old Honus Wagner still playing for them?"

"He quit five or six years back, as I recollect," I said.

"Damn!" said Short Schmidt. "No wonder they ain't won any pennants to speak of."

"*Damn* that John McGraw and his Giants!" added Long Schmidt passionately.

I could see they were bound and determined to talk about baseball for a few hours, so I decided that it was a good time to take my leave of them. "Well," I said, "this has been a fascinating experience, hobnobbing with a couple of flesh-and-blood gods and seeing a lost civilization and all, but I think maybe the time has come for me to depart."

"What makes you think *you're* going anywhere?" demanded Long Schmidt.

"What reason have you got to keep me?" I said. "I told you everything I know about baseball, and nobody's got around to declaring me a god yet."

"First you got to help us get out of here," said Short Schmidt. "After all, fair is fair."

"I don't see nothing fair about it," I said, getting a little hot under the collar.

"Don't look so glum, Jones," said Long Schmidt. "If you actually *do* figure a way to get us out of here, we'll let you scoop up a handful of gems on the way out."

Which of course put a whole new light on things.

I let one of their wives lead me to a little hut, and I lay down in a hammock and divided my attention between her and the problem at hand, spending most of the night tackling first one and then the other. And by morning I had the solution.

I hunted up Melora, who was about as giggly as ever, which is to say not at all, and told her that I had hit upon a way to turn her gods and husbands into a pair of contented stay-at-homes.

"Truly?" she said, her eyes widening.

"Trust me," I said confidently.

"It is almost too much to ask."

"It all depends on you, Melora," I told her.

"What must I do?" she asked.

"I want you to pick up a couple of rubies or emeralds from wherever it is you guys are hiding them, and then go on a little shopping trip to Germiston for me."

I had to explain what I wanted two or three times before she finally understood, and I told her to make sure to take a couple of husky lads along to haul my purchase back.

Then, after she left sometime around noon, I brought out the Good Book and decided to see if I couldn't bring a little of the true religion to these white heathen and get them to cast their false gods out into the cold, just in case my other idea didn't work.

Well, I was at it for the better part of three weeks and no one got converted, but we all had a fine old time singing hymns and trying to live up to the doings and deeds of all them holy men, especially in regard to all the begatting they did.

The Malaloki were fair to middling cooks, and were the first of Roman descent I'd run across who didn't smother everything in tomatoes and mozzarella cheese. The Schmidt brothers had shown them how to make a kind of wine from fermented fruits that didn't taste too good but packed one hell of a punch, and between the eating and the drinking and the begatting I sure couldn't see why they were so all-fired eager to leave.

Twenty days after Melora left she returned, with her two companions lugging a batch of packages. I had them put the stuff into my hut before the brothers saw them, and went to work. When I was done assembling everything, I made sure it all worked and then called Long Schmidt and Short Schmidt over.

"What have you got to show us, Jones?" said Long Schmidt, ducking his head down to get in through my doorway.

"Looks kind of like a radio," said Short Schmidt.

"Shortwave," I said.

"Should that mean something?" asked Long Schmidt.

I held the earphones between them and started cranking the dynamo.

"*The Pirates lead two to nothing in the seventh, and John McGraw is calling Heinie Groh back and is sending Frankie Frisch up to pinch-hit with runners on first and—*"

I pulled a tube out of the set and smashed it on the floor of the hut.

"My God!" wailed Short Schmidt. "What have you done?"

"Nothing much," I said pleasantly. "I got a spare hidden away."

"Where?" screamed Long Schmidt in agonized tones.

"Why, if I told you, it wouldn't be hidden much longer, would it?" I asked.

"Fix it!" screamed Short Schmidt.

"It's *my* radio," I said. "I put it together and I attached it to the dynamo and I even laid six hundred feet of antenna up the side of the crater. I'll fix it when I feel like listening to it again. Right now, though, I'm planning on taking a nap."

"We'll kill you!" bellowed Long Schmidt, tears streaming down his bearded face.

"That ain't going to get you your tube," I said.

"What do you want for it?" said Short Schmidt, getting down on his knees and sobbing a little.

"Oh, nothing much," I answered. "Maybe just my freedom and a handful of gemstones to tide me over during hard times."

"That was to be your reward for getting us out of here," said Long Schmidt accusingly.

"Why not think over your position for a minute?" I said. "You got more wives than you can shake a stick at, you got a couple of cushy lifetime jobs with no heavy lifting, and you got the Pittsburgh Pirates just a couple of huts away. You got more precious stones than anyone ever thought existed, and nice weather, and three squares a day. Are you sure you really *want* to leave?"

They put their heads together and muttered under their breaths for a while. Then Short Schmidt walked over to his own hut and returned a minute later with a big metal box.

"One handful," he said, opening it up. "No more."

I reached in and pulled out a fistful of rubies and sapphires and other such trinkets and stuffed them into my pockets. Then I took them out behind my hut to a little spot I'd marked, dug down about five or six inches with my fingers, and handed them the tube.

"Anything I can do for you two when I reach civilization?" I asked, preparing to take my leave of them while they were fiddling with the shortwave. "Any messages you want me to deliver?"

"Just send a note to our folks back in Pittsburgh telling them we're okay," said Short Schmidt. "And maybe find a way to tell the Pirates they need more left-handed pitching."

Just then the Giants score three runs in the top of the eighth, and I could see that there wasn't much sense in trying to talk to them any longer, as they were spending all their energy calling down their godly wrath on John McGraw, so I took my leave of them.

Melora shot me the first smile I had ever seen from her and walked me to the tunnel and guided me through and didn't even holler when I didn't exactly grab her hand again.

We finally made it to the plateau that the crater sat on. I kissed her good-bye real courtly-like and, with a handsome fortune in my pockets, I set off for civilization with the happy knowledge that me and God would finally be co-landlords of the Tabernacle of Saint Luke.

10. THE LORD OF THE JUNGLE

Me and the Lord spent the next couple of weeks walking in a northerly direction and discussing just how much of our modest fortune should go into the actual building of our tabernacle and how much should be held back for the two of us to live on.

I also learned that having a pocketful of gemstones is a hell of a lot different from wanting one. Now that I was a wealthy man, I was so worried about highwaymen and other rogues robbing a law-abiding citizen like myself that I carefully avoided all cities and military outposts, and even made a huge detour that took me a good forty miles out of my way rather than chance running into a safari that I heard up ahead.

In point of fact, it was all this maneuvering that got me lost. I started hitting one forest after another, which I knew meant I was having some slight difficulty, since British East ain't got no forests, and pretty soon there weren't any gaps at all between them, and then it started doing a little serious nonstop raining, and I soon got to the point where I would gladly have accepted the Lord's share of the stones for a raincoat and a map.

Also, as I walked along I kept getting the feeling that I was being watched by unseen eyes, which in my broad experience on the Dark Continent are the very worst kind of eyes to be watched by. Finally one day I started seeing huge manlike shapes way off in the distance, so I figured I was in gorilla country and spent most of my waking hours trying to recollect whether or not gorillas ate people. I even did a little serious lumbering and grunting in the hope that they might think I was one of them, but then I got to figuring that

I looked pretty feminine as gorillas went and I didn't want to have to fight off no impassioned bull gorillas, or even bull chimpanzees if push came to shove, so I went back to walking like the good-looking God-fearing white man that I am.

I spent another couple of days in the muck and mire of the forest floor and was just about sure I was lost beyond salvation when an arrow thudded home about three inches from my head as I leaned up against a huge old tree. I looked up just in time to see a tall, bronzed white man wearing nothing but a dagger and loincloth step out from behind some bushes, with a bow and a couple of arrows clutched in his right hand.

"What are you doing in my jungle?" he demanded in deep, stern tones.

"Looking for a way out," I told him sincerely.

"And who are you?" he asked, glaring at me.

"The Right Reverend Honorable Doctor Lucifer Jones at your service," I said, flashing him a big Sunday-morning smile. "Preaching and salvation done cheap, with a group rate for funerals."

"Good!" he said, sighing deeply and looking mightily relieved. "I was afraid you might be from Barrow, Phillips, and Smythe."

"Who are they?"

"My British creditors."

"You expect them to follow you here?" I asked.

"You've no idea how firm their resolve can be," he said. "Allow me to introduce myself. I am John Caldwell, Lord Bloomstoke."

"Make up your mind," I said.

"I beg your pardon?"

"Which are you: Caldwell or Bloomstoke?"

"Both. One is a title. Unfortunately, it costs a lot more to support a title these days than it ever used to, and finally I had to flee the country to avoid my creditors and their solicitors."

"But why here?" I asked. "I ain't seen naught but grubworms and an occasional monkey in days."

"I thought I was purchasing an up-to-date plantation," he admitted. "You can imagine my distress when I found out that what I really owned was six square miles of the Ituri Rain Forest."

"Who'd you buy it from?" I asked, just out of politeness.

"A realtor with absolutely impeccable credentials," replied Bloomstoke. "What was his name now? Ah, yes—Von Horst."

"Figgers," I said.

"You know of him?"

"In a manner of speaking," I answered. "How long have you been out here?"

"Four years, as near as I can tell."

"That's a long time to be stuck in the bush," I remarked. "What do you do to keep from going nuts?"

"Oh, I spend a lot of the time talking to my friends," he said.

"Friends?" I repeated. "You got friends stashed away around here?"

"Watch," he said with a smile. Then he put his fingers to his lips and let out a weird whistle, and a couple of minutes later a pair of gorillas broke into a clearing about thirty yards away. Bloomstoke immediately started jabbering at them in some guttural language I hadn't never heard before, and they nodded their heads and disappeared back into the forest.

"Are you telling me they understand you?" I asked.

"Absolutely," he said. "I studied French at Oxford. There's very little difference, except that apes have only the haziest understanding of the future imperfect except as it relates to hunting for grubworms."

"You're pulling my leg, right?"

"Not a bit." He smiled. "If you have any messages for them, I'll be happy to translate for you. Of course, you have to be a little careful with your idioms. For example, if I were to tell them that you thought we were pulling your leg, and I didn't remember to drop half a tone on the double *arrrgeth* sound, they could immediately come over and pull your leg off." He paused. "But aside from such minor technicalities, we have quite excellent conversations. Of course, it's not as if they can discuss Plato's *Republic* with any depth of understanding, but on the other hand they also can't discuss Sartre and Descartes at all, which I for one consider a definite plus."

"And you live with these here gorillas?" I asked.

"Oh, yes," he said happily. "In fact, I've worked my way up into their hierarchy due to my physical prowess. You see, apes fight for their various leadership positions. At this very moment," he added with more than a touch of pride, "I am Assistant to the Second Vice President."

"Now, I would have sworn they had a king," I said, shaking my head in wonderment.

"Oh, they used to, before we started discussing the problems inherent in constitutional monarchies," replied Bloomstoke. "We currently have a very limited republic, but I won't quit until we've established a true socialist state."

"Well, Brother Bloomstoke," I said, "it sure sounds like you've accomplished quite a lot in just four years' time."

"Thank you," he said modestly. "But there's so much to do! My God, do you realize that we haven't even taken the first small steps toward establishing a group medical plan?"

"I would imagine that most of your medical emergencies consist of being et by lions and leopards and the like, and as such would be somewhat beyond the scope of a group plan," I opined.

"True," he admitted. "But you can't just have a bureaucracy and not give it anything to do. That's just plain wasteful. No, Doctor Jones, I appreciate your kind words, truly I do, but there is so much left undone."

"Seems to me you've done more than enough," I said soothingly.

He shook his head sadly. "Even our military establishment can't seem to function efficiently."

"You got a military establishment?" I asked, surprised.

"Of course," he said. "Our economy was in a shambles. We couldn't see any way of bringing it back to life except by gearing up for a little war."

"Who are you going to fight with—elephants?"

"That's not an issue at this point," he said. "When we're geared up and ready, we'll find an enemy."

"Have you considered the possibility that maybe you bit off a little more than you can chew?" I suggested.

"Sometimes it feels that way," he admitted with a deep sigh. "I mean, I speak to them of Romeo and Juliet, or Arthur and Guinevere, and all they want to do is enter into uncomplicated relationships with other apes. That's all right; I can accept that. I really can. But when I try to discuss welfare statism and all they want to do is peel bananas . . ." His voice trailed off, and his handsome face contorted as he fought to hold back a manly little sob.

"Look at the bright side," I said. "You got your health, you ain't sitting in a debtor's prison, and you've actually learned their language."

"I know," he said. "But sometimes I get so frustrated! Do you know what the gorilla word for 'moon' is? *Kablooga! You* try to write a poem and see what the hell rhymes with *kablooga!* In a way it's an even sillier language than French."

"Of course, there ain't no law that says you got to associate with them," I pointed out.

"With all their faults, they're still preferable to men," he replied hotly. "They don't cheat at cards or vote for *laissez-faire* capitalism or mix their drinks . . ."

"I'm just pointing out alternatives," I said.

"I know," he said. "I'm inclined to be emotional these days. I suspect it all goes back to my troubles with Barrow, Phillips, and Smythe."

I was about to make some comforting remark or other when a huge bull gorilla broke cover about two hundred yards away, stared balefully at us for a couple of minutes, and walked off into the bushes.

"That was George," said Bloomstoke. "He's probably trying to let me know tactfully that it's time for a meeting of the Governing Council."

Another gorilla came out of the bushes no more than ten feet away and walked up to me.

"It's just George," explained Bloomstoke calmly. "He's come to see where you are."

"But he was a furlong away just a couple of seconds ago!"

"No, that was a different one," said Bloomstoke.

"You call them both George?" I asked.

"I call them *all* George," he replied. "It helps impart the notion that the state is more important than the individual."

The George that was examining me put his face about two inches from mine and glared into my eyes with his own little bloodshot ones. His teeth were sort of rotten, and his breath wasn't much better, but as much as I wanted to turn my head away I thought it best not to make any real sudden moves.

At last George turned to Bloomstoke and jabbered something. Bloomstoke jabbered back and then turned to me.

"George wants to know if you're a Whig or a Tory," he said.

"I got to admit it ain't a subject over which I've pondered many long and burdensome hours," I answered.

They jabbered back and forth again, and finally George gave me a little snarl and went back off into the jungle.

"I told him you were an anarchist," said Bloomstoke. "It was easier than explaining why you choose not to exercise your franchise."

"Actually, I used to exercise the tar out of it when I was back in the States," I said. "I'd vote early and often for whichever candidate was quick on the draw with a ten-spot or a little pure Kentucky bourbon."

"An interesting notion," remarked Bloomstoke, "and one I may have to introduce very shortly. You see, we've got a sheriff and a marshal and a police force, but the concept of lawbreaking is totally unknown to them, which makes for more waste than usual among our officeholders."

Well, it was all too complicated for me, and I just walked along in silence while Bloomstoke outlined his grandiose plans to me. He must have been running off at the mouth for the better part of an hour when we heard a gunshot off in the distance.

"More territorial aggrandizement!" he muttered, his eyes gleaming. "I'll have to put a stop to this." He turned to me. "How are you at racing through the treeways?"

"You mean swinging on vines like unto a monkey?" I asked.

He nodded.

"Brother Bloomstoke, I got troubles enough just keeping on the trail as it meanders along through the bush, and *that's* with the comforting knowledge that if I slip and fall I'll hit the ground in less than twenty or thirty seconds and probably won't bounce. Maybe you'd best race off ahead of me."

"I'd like to, but I can't leave you alone with the apes," he replied. "They've never seen an anarchist before, and there's no telling what they might do."

And with that, he cupped his hands over his mouth and gave a scream that would have woke such dead as weren't otherwise occupied at the time. I couldn't figure out what was going on until about two minutes later, when a huge elephant thundered up out of the bush, crushing trees right and left and skidding to a halt directly in front of Bloomstoke.

"Goola, my friend," he said, stepping forward and petting the elephant on the trunk while I decided that the whole proceedings made a lot more sense when watched from behind a large tree. "Come on out, Doctor Jones," he called. "Goola will provide us with transportation."

"How do I know that I won't provide old Goola here with a little snack?" I asked, for to my eyes Goola was looking decidedly eleven-o'clockish, an opinion that was strengthened by the loud rumbling noises that his belly was making.

"Goola will do what I tell him to do," said Bloomstoke firmly. "Now come out so that he can see you."

"I don't know about this," I said from behind my tree. "He can't eat what he can't see."

"Elephants are herbivores," said Bloomstoke.

"They're also very nearsighted," I pointed out. "Maybe I look like a fig tree to him."

"If you don't come out instantly, I'll simply leave you behind," he said.

I quickly discussed my options with my Silent Partner, and we decided that being left behind was—very minimally—the less desirable of two admittedly depressing alternatives, so I slowly left the protection of my tree and edged, a step at a time, over toward Goola.

"Let him smell the back of your hand," said Bloomstoke.

I held out my hand and Goola took a good whiff, almost pulling my arm out of the socket in the process.

"Good!" said Bloomstoke vigorously. "Now we're all friends. Goola, lift us up!"

Goola pawed the ground three times with his right front foot.

"No, Goola!" said Bloomstoke. "*Lift!*"

Goola rolled over on his back and closed his eyes.

"Idiot!" snapped Bloomstoke. I kept feeling we should throw him a fish or something, but my companion stalked off furiously. "Come on, Jones, we'll walk!"

When we got about a hundred yards away Goola trumpeted six or seven times and stood on his head. Then we took a hard left around a wait-a-bit thorn tree and I couldn't see him anymore, though we could hear him for another ten minutes.

We followed an old rhino trail in the direction of the gunshots, and in about half an hour Bloomstoke held out his arm, practically decapitating me as I walked by him, and when I fell to the ground, gurgling and gasping for air, he put a forefinger to his lips.

"Silence!" he whispered.

Well, I would have told him what I thought of his silence, but I was a little preoccupied with choking to death, so I merely glared at him and quietly urged the Lord to strike him either dead or mute, whichever came first.

I got my breath back and stood up just in time to see Bloomstoke stride out of the bushes into a clearing to confront a kind of smallish white man dressed all in khaki.

"Who are you that invades my jungle?" Bloomstoke demanded.

"I'm Capturing Clyde Calhoun," said the white man, not looking the least bit scared or startled. "And you are either the strongest white man or the puniest gorilla I've ever laid eyes on."

"What is your business here?" said Bloomstoke ominously.

"Business?" laughed Calhoun. "Ain't you never read my books or seen my movies? I'm Capturing Clyde! I go out after the most dangerous animals in the world—except for redheads named Thelma—and bring 'em back alive, and put 'em in my circus or turn 'em over to zoos or gourmet chefs or other interested parties."

"What animals do you seek?"

"Gorillas," said Calhoun. "Thought I'd bring back fifteen or twenty of 'em before they're all extinct."

"I distinctly heard the reports of a powerful gun," said Bloomstoke.

"You bet your boots you did," said Calhoun, holding up a Lee-Enfield .303 military rifle. "Or at least you would if you were wearing any boots."

"I thought you told me that you brought them back alive," said Bloomstoke accusingly.

"Maybe I should reword that a bit," said Calhoun. "Them what I bring back *is* alive. I just take old Betsy here and aim right betwixt their eyes and fire away. Anything still breathing gets captured and civilized."

"Where's your camp?" asked Bloomstoke.

"About eight miles behind me," said Calhoun. "You can't miss it. I've got two hundred porters, a dozen trackers, ten cooks, a couple of translators, and forty-three veterinarians."

I stepped out of the clearing next to Bloomstoke.

"What the hell are you?" demanded Calhoun.

"The Right Reverend Doctor Lucifer Jones, at your service," I said.

"You got any good funeral ceremonies for hippos?" he asked.

"I ain't never tried my hand at one," I admitted.

"Then you'll have to be at someone else's service, Reverend Jones," he said. "I got a little too enthused down by the river this morning."

"You planning on going back to Nairobi anytime in the near future?" I asked him.

"Soon as I pick up my gorillas," he said.

"Mind if I tag along with you?"

"Why not?" he said. "What the hell are you doing out here in the Congo anyway?"

"I've mostly been concentrating on being lost," I said.

"How about you?" he said to Bloomstoke. "You coming back to Nairobi too?"

"This is my jungle," said Bloomstoke, folding his arms across his massive chest. "I will not leave it, and you will not hunt in it."

"Do you know who you're talking to?" roared Calhoun. "I'm Capturing Clyde, by God, and I'll hunt where I want!"

"This jungle belongs to me, and I will not allow you to molest my gorillas," reported Bloomstoke.

"What kind of pervert do you take me for?" said Calhoun. "I don't want to molest them! I want to capture them!"

"No," said Bloomstoke. "Now I want you to leave my jungle."

"Who says it's *your* jungle anyway?" demanded Calhoun.

Bloomstoke reached inside his loincloth and whipped out a pair of folded documents, which he handed to Calhoun.

"Son of a bitch!" exclaimed Calhoun after he had read them. "I didn't know they could sell a jungle."

"Neither did I," said Bloomstoke morosely.

"Who'd you buy it from?" asked Calhoun.

"A man named Von Horst."

"Figgers."

"Why does everyone say that?" asked Bloomstoke.

"I'd tell you, but it brings back too many unpleasant memories," said Calhoun. "I don't suppose you'd consider renting me a little section of your jungle, with maybe an option to buy?"

"I could use the money," admitted Bloomstoke. "But I'd have to present your proposal to the tribe and get their approval, and they're very leery of anything that reeks of capitalism."

"Tribe?" asked Calhoun. "What tribe? I didn't know there were any natives in this region."

"This tribe is a little more native than most," I said.

"No," concluded Bloomstoke, shaking his head sadly. "I'll never get the Ruling Council to buy it."

"Would it help if I told them they could retain the mineral rights?" asked Calhoun.

"I doubt it," said Bloomstoke truthfully.

"All right," said Calhoun. "I've got another proposition. I'm being paid four thousand pounds for every gorilla I capture. If you'll let me hunt in your jungle and give me a helping hand, I'll split the take fifty-fifty with you."

"How many gorillas do you need?" asked Bloomstoke.

"About twenty."

"And I owe Barrow, Phillips, and Smythe thirty-eight thousand pounds," he mused. Then he shook his head again. "No! I just can't! John D. Rockefeller or J. P. Morgan might have understood, but Karl Marx would come back and haunt me."

"And George would eat you," I added.

"What the hell are you guys talking about?" asked Calhoun.

"Let me speak to them about accepting a short-term lease on the jungle," said Bloomstoke, grabbing an overhanging branch and pulling himself up on it. "Maybe I can show them that Fabian socialism doesn't necessarily preclude the validity of certain capitalistic principles." He leaped into the air, caught a low-hanging vine, and was soon racing through the treetops to meet with the tribe.

"Tell me something, Reverend Jones," said Calhoun, leaning against a tree and lighting up a pipe.

"If I can," I said amicably.

"When Americans go crazy they beat up their wives and spend their life savings on booze, which at least keeps their women on their toes and puts a little money back into the economy. And when Irishmen go crackers, they go off and join the IRA and help keep down the population of a very crowded little island." He paused thoughtfully. "So how come whenever Englishmen go nuts then run around naked in tropical climates?"

I allowed as to how I didn't know, but it did seem to be the case, at least in my experience. He pulled out a small metal flask and offered me a swig, and we got to talking about one thing and another, passing the time of day very pleasantly, when suddenly we heard a horrible sound away off in the distance.

"What is it?" asked Calhoun.

"I can't rightly tell," I answered.

"Sounds like a bunch of savage voices screaming in fury," he said, putting his flask away.

A moment later we heard a noise overhead, and saw Bloomstoke dropping down from one branch to another until he finally landed right next to us on the ground.

"Hurry!" he cried. "We've no time to waste!"

"What are you talking about, Brother Bloomstoke?" I asked.

"We've got to get out of here!"

"But what happened?" I persisted.

"They decided that I was a closet imperialist and threw me out of the party! *Me*, who brought them a fourteen-year agricultural recovery plan!"

"What's he talking about, Reverend?" asked Calhoun.

"I think he's saying that his visa's been revoked and he is in some danger of being deported," I said, falling into step behind Bloomstoke as he lit out for the east. "Or worse yet, detained without right of counsel."

"Are you sure we have to run?" panted Calhoun, joining me.

"I'm sure *I* have to run," I replied. "You do whatever you think is best."

We made it to Calhoun's camp in about three hours. The gorillas lined up in a huge semi-circle just out of rifle range and kept screaming things at us, which Bloomstoke translated as "capitalist swine" and "war-mongering imperialists" and "running dogs". Every now and then one of them would call us "ugly naked apes who didn't have the brains to turn over a rotten log and find a handful of succulent grubworms," at which Bloomstoke would smile and inform us that obviously the entire tribe was not yet radicalized.

By dawn the next morning it was apparent that the gorillas weren't going to come no closer and that Bloomstoke wasn't going to let no one go hunting in his jungle, so Calhoun announced that we would be leaving for Nairobi in an hour or so. Bloomstoke gave out that peculiar scream of his, and a few minutes later old Goola came lumbering out of the jungle.

"Don't shoot him," ordered Bloomstoke, as Calhoun raised his rifle.

"But he'll trample us!" said Calhoun.

"Am I not Master of the Jungle?" said Bloomstoke with a confident smile. He raised his hand and Goola came to a sudden stop.

"He does whatever you tell him to?" asked Calhoun, suddenly interested.

Bloomstoke nodded.

"You ever give any serious thought to appearing in the circus?" continued Calhoun.

"I'd need thirty-eight thousand pounds," said Bloomstoke.

"Out of the question!" said Calhoun.

"That would include the elephant."

"Let's see what he can do," said Calhoun, scratching his head.

Bloomstoke walked up to the pachyderm. "Goola—sit!" he commanded.

Goola picked Bloomstoke up with his trunk and deposited the jungle lord on the back of his neck.

"We'll work on that," said Bloomstoke hastily. "Put me down, Goola."

Goola pawed the ground three times with his right front foot, while Calhoun snorted in derision and walked away.

"I could be an aerialist!" Bloomstoke called after him. "I'm really good at swinging from tree to tree."

"I'll think about it," said Calhoun.

"Or a sharpshooter!" continued Bloomstoke. "I'm a crack shot with a bow and arrow. Damn you, Goola—put me the hell down!"

Well, they spent most of the day dickering, but the upshot of it all was that Calhoun already had a flock of aerialists, and besides, it would cost too much to lug a bunch of trees and vines around the countryside and erect them under the big top. Also, people didn't pay top dollar to watch bows-and-arrow marksmen unless they were with a Wild West Show, which was one of the kinds of shows that Calhoun didn't run.

"Tell you what I'll do," said Calhoun at last. "You teach that elephant five tricks by the time we hit Nairobi and I'll pay you thirty-eight thousand pounds to go on tour with my circus for two years."

"And if I don't?" asked Bloomstoke.

"Then I'll buy him outright for ten thousand, and you can hire on as an animal attendant for standard wages."

"Capitalist pig!" muttered Bloomstoke, but he shook on it.

Well, I never saw an elephant not learn so many tricks in my life as I did during the month it took us to get from the Congo to Kenya. Bloomstoke would tell him to stand up, and he'd roll over. Bloomstoke would tell him to lie down, and he'd speak. Bloomstoke would tell him to speak, and he'd count with his foot. When we were two days out of Nairobi it was pretty obvious that Bloomstoke was going to come out on the short end of the deal, so I walked over to him after everyone else was asleep.

"You been going about this all wrong, Brother Bloomstoke," I said, taking him off to where we wouldn't disturb nobody.

"What do you mean, Doctor Jones?" he asked.

"Look, we all agree that old Goola, if he ain't out-and-out retarded, has at least got a serious learning disability, right?" I said.

Bloomstoke nodded.

"But he's also a good-hearted critter who's eager to please, even if he don't know what the hell you're talking about."

"What are you getting at?" asked Bloomstoke.

"Why not give him commands in French or ape or some other foreign tongue?" I suggested. "Then, no matter what he does next, praise him and act like it was just what you had in mind."

"That's immoral," he said sternly.

"Well, personally I find it a lot less immoral than poverty," I said. "But if you disagree, why, that's your right. Just forget I ever suggested it."

The next morning Bloomstoke called Calhoun over and gave Goola a dozen terse commands in apeish, and shortly thereafter signed a thirty-eight-thousand-pound contract.

As for me, I left Bloomstoke and Calhoun and their animals behind me and, still loaded down with gemstones, went off to build my tabernacle in the fair city of Nairobi.

11. THE BEST LITTLE TABERNACLE IN NAIROBI

If you walk through present-day Nairobi and ask around, you can probably still find three or four old-timers who remember the Tabernacle of Saint Luke, and will be happy to talk to you about it.

So I think, in all fairness, that you ought to hear *my* side of the story too.

I entered town a couple of hours after I'd left Bloomstoke and Calhoun, and walked right into the first real estate office I could find, not that there were a whole mess of them cluttering up the place. In fact, except for the New Stanley and Norfolk hotels, there wasn't an awful lot of anything cluttering up the place.

Anyway, I told the gent in charge that I wanted to purchase a little stretch of land somewhere near the center of town with the purpose of building my tabernacle there, and he explained to me that while he could certainly sell me the land, there was a lumber shortage and construction costs had shot up through the roof—or they would have, if anyone could have afforded a roof for them to shoot up through.

"I got an awful lot of money," I told him. "Of course, on the other hand, the Lord teaches us to be thrifty. It poses quite a little problem."

"There is an alternative, Doctor Jones," he said.

"Such as?"

"Why not purchase an existing structure?" he suggested. "It would certainly be less expensive than erecting a comparable building, and you'd have the added advantage of being able to take possession and move in immediately."

"Well, now, that's right good thinking, brother," I said. "And I opine as to how I'll do just that. Why don't you hunt me up the biggest building that's for sale?"

"Well, Doctor Jones, sir," he said, "I'm thoroughly acquainted with all the property currently listed with our agency and I don't think the largest building is exactly the one you're looking for."

"Is the structure sound?" I asked.

"Yes."

"No termites or dry rot?"

"No, but . . ."

"Then I want it," I told him decisively. "Have the papers ready to sign, and I'll be back as soon as I convert these here jewels and gems into coin of the realm."

And, as the Lord is my witness, that was absolutely all that got said by anybody to anybody.

I mean, how the hell was I to know that the biggest building for sale in Nairobi happened to be the Cock and Bull Tavern and Lounge, or that the Cock and Bull Tavern and Lounge wasn't exactly what it appeared to be?

In fact, the first inkling I had was when I moseyed over to it after signing the papers and damned near got trampled in a mad rush of British civil servants who were stopping off for a little refreshment on their way home from a hard day of running the country. A couple of ladies in high-necked dresses were standing just outside the doorway, passing out pamphlets and singing hymns.

"Good day to you, sisters," I said, walking up to them.

"It won't be a good day until this sinful palace of depravity is closed forever!" said one of them. "Won't you take some of our literature, sir?"

"No, thank you, sister," I said. "I never read anything except the Good Book. But perhaps you might tell me why you've singled out this lovely building from amongst all the other buildings in Nairobi?"

"It's not the building, sir," said the other. "It's what goes on inside it: sin and more sin!"

She raised her voice a little in her excitement, and as a result two men who were walking on the other side of the street heard her and made a beeline for the Cock and Bull.

"Sinners!" cried the first woman after them. "Vile, depraved men!"

"Listen, sisters," I said. "Since I'm a man of the cloth, maybe I'd best go inside and see if I can put the fear of God into some of these sinners. But I want you to keep standing here by the door and telling everyone who comes by what a terrible den of iniquity this is."

"Oh, we will, Reverend!" they cried in unison.

"Especially the men," I said.

They nodded, their eyes aglow with a sense of purpose, and I walked through the doorway. The bar looked like any other bar in town, with lion and leopard and kudu and buffalo heads hanging from the walls, and a bunch of Maasai pots serving as spittoons. And being the uncannily sharp observer that I am, I didn't have to see more than six or seven ladies walking around in their unmentionables before I figured out that either the fans were broken or the Cock and Bull sold a little more than just liquid refreshments.

I wandered around the main floor a little, enjoying the smells of perfume and incense that wafted on the air and admiring the velvet wallpaper that came with the building. Then I bumped into still another young lady who was dressed for extremely warm weather.

"Good evening, sister," I said.

"You're wearing your Sunday-go-to-meeting clothes a little early in the week, aren't you?" she asked.

"Don't let my clothes upset you none," I said pleasantly.

"If mine don't upset you, yours sure won't upset me," she said. "What can I do for you, Padre—a little something in the missionary position?"

"You might tell me how to find whoever's in charge here," I said.

"You must mean Mademoiselle Markoff," she said, gesturing toward a room at the top of a nearby staircase.

I thanked her, walked up, and knocked on the door. There was no answer, so I opened it and found myself facing a blonde woman with a figure that Knute Rockne would have traded all four of Notre Dame's horsemen for. Her arms, thighs, shoulders, and neck all bore a right startling resemblance to those of Lord Bloomstoke's friends and companions. She was dressed, or rather wrapped, in a blue satin harem outfit which looked kind of silly and would have looked even sillier if she hadn't appeared so menacing. She was lying on her side on a fur rug, sipping a tall drink through a straw and holding a huge cigar in her free hand. A couple of young women, also done up in satin and wearing huge feathers in their hair, were standing behind her and waving ostrich-feather fans over her sweating body.

"What is it?" she said in a very deep voice.

"Allow me to introduce myself," I said. "I'm the Right Reverend Doctor Lucifer Jones. How's the concierge business these days?"

"Another reformer," she said wearily, looking up from her drink.

"Begging your pardon, Madam Markoff," I said, "but what I mostly am is a landlord."

"Call me Mademoiselle Markoff. I'm too young and pretty to be a madam—or don't you agree?" she said ominously.

"I agree absolutely, Mademoiselle," I said, taking a step backward.

"Good," she said, simpering in A below middle C. "Now what's all this about being a landlord?"

I pulled out the papers and showed them to her.

"Oh, shit!" she said, tossing them back to me. "When will you want us to clear out of here?"

"Mademoiselle Markoff, you cut me to the quick!" I said sincerely. "Tossing all them sweet innocent young ladies out into the cold would hardly constitute an act of Christian charity, especially considering how many customers we got lined up downstairs."

Her eyebrows shot up for just a second, and then she gave me a great big grin that started at one ear and ended just short of the other. "Doctor Jones," she said, "it looks like you've bought yourself a whorehouse."

"I don't think so, Mademoiselle," I said. "It just wouldn't appear right, me being a man of the cloth and all."

"I don't think I follow you," she said, taking a deep drag on her cigar, blowing the smoke out through her nostrils, and sipping two-thirds of the drink up through her straw.

"What I'm saying is that I just don't think a man in my position should own a whorehouse. Of course, as I see it, *renting* a whorehouse to someone else is a whole different kettle of fish."

"Ah!" she said, her grin getting even bigger, exposing a flock of gold molars along the sides. "And what will you be wanting?"

"Well, I sure wouldn't want to appear greedy or nothing," I said. "But first of all, I'll need a room downstairs for my tabernacle."

"And what else?" she persisted.

"Half," I said.

"Damn!" she snapped. "You're no better than the last one! Listen to me, Doctor Jones: these are cultured young women here, performing a necessary if demeaning social service."

"And just what would it take to make them feel less demeaned?" I asked.

"Sixty percent ought to do it," said Mademoiselle Markoff.

"Fifty-five," I said.

"Done!" she said.

We shook on it.

"How much do *you* get, by the way?" I asked while trying to urge a little blood back into my hand.

"Half of their take," she said without batting an eye.

"Well, the Good Lord teaches us to practice moderation in all things, so I guess that includes generosity for these poor, socially downtrodden young ladies," I said.

"You're *cute*," said Mademoiselle Markoff, allowing a lock of blonde hair to fall provocatively over one beady little red eye.

"Why, thank you kindly," I said, backing off another step.

"Come sit down next to me and have a drink, Doctor Jones," she said, patting the rug beside her. "I have a feeling that you and I are going to get along just fine."

I was about to reply when two gunshots echoed through the building. They were followed by a bunch of screams and the sound of footsteps running up and down the corridors and stairs, and finally a tall, bearded man in a police uniform burst into the room.

"Mademoiselle Markoff!" he bellowed. "He did it again! It's got to stop!"

"Beggin' your pardon, brother," I said, "but what seems to be the problem?"

"Who the hell are you?" he demanded.

"The Right Reverend Doctor Lucifer Jones," I said. "I happen to be the new landlord."

He looked at Mademoiselle Markoff, who nodded.

"Pleased to meet you, Doctor Jones," he said, extending his hand. "I am Lieutenant Nigel Todd of the Nairobi Police. Are you aware of the exact nature of the establishment you have just purchased?"

"Everyone who works here is just doing what they can to uplift the spirit of Man, each in his or her own special way," I said, taking his hand.

"Not quite everyone," said Todd grimly.

"What happened?" I asked. "Surely them two ladies out front didn't come in and shoot the place up? I'll have to explain to them that the Good Book dwells upon numerous painted women with loving care and in considerable detail."

"It's your bouncer," said Todd.

"What's the matter with him?" I asked.

"He keeps shooting the customers."

"Not before they've paid, I hope?" I said.

"I must tell you, Doctor Jones," continued Todd, "it's getting harder and harder to tolerate this kind of thing. I'm as liberal as the next man, but he simply can't be allowed to go around shooting people whenever he pleases. After all, this isn't the frontier anymore, and it is getting very difficult, to say nothing of expensive, to keep such unfortunate events quiet."

"Expensive?" I said.

"Expensive," he replied, putting his hand into his pocket and jingling his change, just like a high-class waiter or bellboy.

"We'll take care of the expenses later," I said. "In the meantime, since it is in both our interests for my only tenant to remain in business, I think maybe I'd better have a little chat with the bouncer in question."

"I'll have him sent right in," said Todd.

"Let me ask you something," I said to Mademoiselle Markoff after Lieutenant Todd had gone to get the bouncer. "If he's been shooting people right along, why didn't you fire him weeks ago?"

"I did," said Mademoiselle Markoff. "But he likes it here. He's working for free."

"Is he a *large* man?" I asked, suddenly wondering at the wisdom of this proposed meeting. "Much of a temper?"

"No," she replied. "In point of fact, he's really quite small."

"Fine," I said, sitting on the rug beside her and lighting one of her cigars. "Then let's solve this little problem once and for all."

A moment later there was a soft knock at the door.

"Come in," said Mademoiselle Markoff.

The door opened and an olive-skinned little man with sad eyes, a dapper-looking suit, and slicked-down black hair walked in.

"Rodent!" I exclaimed. "What the hell are you doing here?"

"Doctor Jones!" he said in that nasal voice of his. "I might ask the very same question of a man of the cloth. It has been quite some time since we have seen each other, but I seem to recall that the circumstances of our parting were not such that I truly wish to continue our relationship."

"I'm afraid you ain't got a hell of a lot of choice in the matter," I said. "I'm the new landlord. What's all this I hear about you shooting up a customer?"

"It was an act of self-defense, I assure you," he said.

"Again?" snorted Mademoiselle Markoff.

"What were the circumstances?" I asked.

"I was climbing up the stairs and a rather large man was coming down, and he wouldn't get out of the way."

"So you shot him?" I demanded.

"What else was I to do?" asked the Rodent with a shrug. "He was much larger than I am."

"That's it?" I said. "That's the whole story, and you call that self-defense?"

"Certainly," said the Rodent. "I view it as *preventive* self-defense. After all, I would hardly have been in any condition to defend myself if he had pushed me down the stairs."

"Rodent, you just can't go around doing things like that!" I snapped. "You're not even on the payroll!"

"The very point I should like to discuss with you," he said with an apologetic little smile.

"Oh?" said Mademoiselle Markoff and me in unison.

"Yes. I have been working for free for the past seven weeks, during which time I have had to defend my life on no less than five separate occasions. Surely I deserve to go back on the payroll after having undergone such privation."

"I don't know exactly how to get this through to you, Rodent," I said, "but if you don't stop shooting people we ain't gonna *have* no payroll."

With no warning at all he reached inside his coat, and I dove for cover behind Mademoiselle Markoff. When I didn't hear any shots, I cautiously raised my head above her ample flanks to see what was going on.

The Rodent was carefully dabbing at his face with a delicate white handkerchief.

"Damn it all, you got to stop making sudden moves like that!" I snapped, rising to my feet and brushing myself off.

"My deepest apologies," said the Rodent, hiding his face behind the handkerchief. "I had no desire to scare or startle you. Now, I believe we were talking about my salary?"

I was half inclined to argue the point with him, but I figured if I did he'd just go reaching into his coat again and since no one could ever be quite sure what he'd pull out, it made more sense to put him back on the payroll.

"But with one stipulation," I told him.

"Yes?" he said gently.

"You shoot anyone else who doesn't take a shot at you first and you're fired. You understand?"

"I understand," he said in a way that led me to think that there was yet another question to be asked, like did he agree, but I decided to let it pass.

"Where do you know him from?" asked Mademoiselle Markoff when the Rodent had left the room.

"Oh, I knew him back in Dar-es-Salaam a couple of years ago," I said. "He tried to get me to finance a highly illegal operation, but being a man of strong moral character I managed to resist the temptation."

"How clever of you," she purred, taking another deep drag on her cigar. "Wouldn't you care to join me again on the rug?"

"I'd sure love to do that, Mademoiselle Markoff," I said, crossing my fingers behind my back, "but it really wouldn't look too good, me being a man of the cloth and all."

"So who's to know?" she whispered, shooting me a wink that would have given a lesser man nightmares for a month.

"Well, for starters, you got two of your young ladies standing right here swiping at your fair body with their fans," I said.

"That's all right," she said. "The one on the left is totally trustworthy, and the other one is inattentive to a fault."

"I'd still feel bad about it, this being my first night on the job, so to speak," I said. "Besides, I still got lots of work to do."

"Such as?"

"Well, first of all, starting tomorrow the Cock and Bull signs are all coming down, and this place will be going under the name of the Tabernacle of Saint Luke. Then I've got to hunt up Lieutenant Nigel Todd and make such arrangements as may be necessary to hush up this unfortunate act of self-defense that the Rodent was undoubtedly forced into against such meager will as he possesses. And finally, I left a couple of little ladies at the front door to scare away undesirables and the like, and I want to make sure they know they'll be welcome any time they want to come around here. So as you can see, I'm just gonna be too busy for any romantic entanglements tonight."

"Perhaps tomorrow, then," she said, licking her lips with a tongue that could have taken the hide off a rhinoceros.

"Why not?" I said as I left the room. I was still coming up with reasons why not when I got hold of Lieutenant Todd and made such restitution as was required to keep the whole unhappy affair of the Rodent under his hat. Then I introduced myself to the bartender, a cadaverous Armenian named Irving, and told him to get a sign painter out the first thing in the morning.

I took a room in the New Stanley Hotel, tried unsuccessfully to buy the painting of Nellie Willoughby that they had hanging over the bar, and finally turned in for a good night's sleep. It seemed like a waste of money, since I owned about twenty rooms with beds over at my tabernacle, but I just had a feeling that I'd be much happier in the New Stanley until me and Mademoiselle Markoff came to an understanding betwixt ourselves.

When I showed up the next afternoon I saw that the signs were already changed. When I went into the bar to tell Irving what a good job he had done, Mademoiselle Markoff was waiting for me, wearing a red gown that would have been roomy on most Siamese triplets, but that fit her so snugly that I could see the huge mole on her left thigh right through it.

"Good morning, Lucifer," she breathed.

"Good day to you," I said.

"I was wondering if you'd like to come up to my office for a few minutes so we can go over some figures?" she tittered in a voice like unto an opera baritone.

"Well, I'd like to, I truly would," I said, "but being a man of the cloth and all, I think it would be more appropriate for me to start setting up my tabernacle now."

There wasn't much she could say to that, so she settled for offering to help me, and then there wasn't much *I* could say to that, so I just thanked her and we went down the hall to the large room that she had put aside for my use.

It was kind of dirty, and needed a new coat of paint, and the ceiling was caving in, and there were only two chairs, but it suited my needs just fine, since I thought it might take the preaching business a good four or five years to grow to where I needed better quarters, or even more chairs.

On the other hand, it seemed to be the one place where I was reasonably safe from Mademoiselle Markoff's advances, so I decided to throw myself into its remodeling with a vengeance. She and I worked side by side replastering the ceiling and staining the walls and putting a parquet floor in and building an altar and getting some stained glass to replace the old dirty windows and building a number of pews so that the room could actually hold about thirty people.

This took us the better part of two months, during which time the Rodent didn't shoot anyone else, and business was booming. Lieutenant Todd stopped by for his payoff every other night, and the police left us alone, and the two little ladies kept screaming in glowing detail about what was going on inside the Tabernacle of Saint Luke, and pretty soon the editor of the local paper started coming by with Lieutenant Todd and getting an occasional gift of one kind or another, and shortly thereafter we were never again mentioned in the papers.

In fact, everything was going smooth as silk except that I was running out of excuses for keeping out of Mademoiselle Markoff's room and going over figures with her, so I worked an extra week building me a pulpit and when she still kept hanging around I took to preaching a good eight or nine hours a day, interspersing my lectures with the latest race results from Johannesburg and some soccer scores from Cairo so as to appeal to a wider audience. I got to admit that we didn't do much off-the-street business, but most of the girls and some of the customers would wander in from time to time and I'd tell 'em what terrible sinners they were and how carnal knowledge was old Satan's foothold in the world of fast women and shameless men and how they'd well better repent right quick, and then they'd go back to their rooms feeling all refreshed and cleansed of soul. In fact, just so's they'd know the Lord was a forgiving type, I began pardoning them for future sins as well as past ones, kind of getting a couple of pages ahead in the heavenly ledger, so to speak.

It got a little difficult to keep finding new subject matter, especially after I'd whipped through a three-day lecture on Solomon's seven hundred or so wives and what he probably did with 'em, but every time I'd think of slipping out for a little liquid refreshment or some other kind of tension easer, I'd look up and there'd be Mademoiselle Markoff sitting in the first pew, staring unblinkingly at me. I really don't think she missed a single sermon I gave during the whole time the Tabernacle of Saint Luke was in business.

I'd been there almost seven months and had just polished off my two hundredth sermon when Lieutenant Nigel Todd, looking agitated as all get-out, stormed into the tabernacle and pulled me off toward a corner.

"Jones, he's done it again!" he snapped.

"Who's done what?" I asked.

"Your friend the Rodent seems to have fallen off the wagon, so to speak," said Todd.

"How did it happen this time?"

"He claims it was self-defense as to who was going to use the sink in the men's room first," said Todd.

"Is the man hurt badly?" I asked.

"I don't believe he felt the last five bullets at all," said Todd.

"Well, at least he ain't suffering unduly," I said. "Why not bring him in here and let me run through a little funeral prayer or two for him?"

"You seem to be missing the point of all this," said Todd. "I'm going to have to arrest the Rodent and lock him up for a good long time."

"Surely we can work something out," I said, putting an arm around his shoulder. "It's not as if we want him to keep working here or nothing like that. I mean, if he shoots enough customers sooner or later we're not going to have any live ones left. But I sure hate to see him go to jail, him being an employee and an old friend of mine and such."

"I'm not a totally unreasonable man," said Lieutenant Todd, starting to jingle the coins in his pocket. "What exactly did you have in mind for him?"

"Well, it just seems a shame that the government will have to feed and care for him. Surely there must be something he can do to repay his debt to society."

"What's he good at?" asked Todd.

"Well, now, that's where we got a little problem," I admitted. "What he's mostly good at, so far as I can tell, is shooting people."

"It may have escaped your notice, Doctor Jones," said Todd, "but that is the very talent we tend to arrest people for these days."

"Do you ever hang 'em?" I asked as my Silent Partner smacked me right between the eyes with a great big revelation.

"From time to time," said Todd.

"Any law says you can't shoot 'em instead?" I said.

"None that I know of," admitted Todd.

"Then why not offer the Rodent a job as your official executioner?" I suggested.

"I have to admit he'd be pretty efficient," mused Todd.

"He'd work cheap too," I said. "Especially once you outlined the nature of his job and the alternatives to accepting it."

"If he's going to go around shooting people, I suppose it does make a certain degree of sense to have him on our side," said Todd. "But I just don't know . . ." He jingled the coins in his pocket a little louder.

I pulled out a wad of bills big enough to assuage Lieutenant Todd's doubts (and to choke a fair-sized horse into the bargain), had a little chat with the Rodent, and saw him off on his way to the first honest job he'd had in years.

Nothing much of interest happened for the next couple of weeks and I fell back into my established routine. Then one day I noticed that Mademoiselle Markoff had put aside her satin wrappings and was now wearing a conservative business suit. A couple of days later she started wearing a severely tailored high-necked black dress, and all her facial makeup was missing, a fact which must have thrown two or three notions shops into bankruptcy in one fell swoop. Then, a few days after that, she started singing the hymns so loud that the paying customers began complaining.

I was pleased to see that she was taking my preaching so much to heart, but I still kept my distance whenever I was outside of the tabernacle. One day, though, I passed her in the hall and for the first time within my memory she didn't even grab at me.

This turn of events made my life just about perfect and I determined then and there to check out the performance of some of my tenants, just to make sure they weren't being more than normally sinful and to offer them dispensation in case they felt a little adventurous.

So that night, after I had completed my evening sermon (which, as I recall, had something to do with the sin of lusting after your neighbors' wives when you could be spending your time with some pleasant bachelor ladies at the Tabernacle of Saint Luke), I wandered up to the second floor and, not wishing to spend too much time reforming all these sinful painted women individually, decided to invite three of them into a room at once.

I was just on the verge of showing them what old Onan was missing when suddenly the door burst open and Lieutenant Nigel Todd walked in.

"You ain't real strong on knocking or announcing yourself, are you, Brother Todd?" I said irritably, wrapping a blanket around myself while the girls scrambled for cover.

"I have no choice, Doctor Jones," he said. "I'm afraid I'm going to have to shutter this establishment."

"What the hell are you talking about?" I demanded. "And how come you ain't jingling your change the way you usually do when we get onto this subject?"

"Because this isn't something we can work out between ourselves," he said. "I've got a court order closing you down." He tossed it onto the bed for me to see.

"But we got nothing but happy, satisfied customers!" I protested. "Who'd be low and dastardly enough to have the judge sign something like this?"

"I'll take credit for it," said Mademoiselle Markoff, appearing in the doorway.

"*You?*" I said. "But why?"

"You've shown me the light, Lucifer," she said with a strange kind of glow on her face. "I've been listening to you preach the Word for more than half a year now, and reading the Good Book every night, and you've shown me the error of my ways."

"What about all these poor innocent girls who ain't quite seen the error of *their* ways yet?" I demanded. "How are they gonna make a living if you stop them from selling the one commodity they know anything about?"

"I'm starting a soup kitchen on the outskirts of town," said Mademoiselle Markoff. "I'll be helping poor downtrodden sinners and derelicts on both sides of the counter, praise God!"

"But what will become of my tabernacle?" I screamed.

"You've been blessed with the call, Lucifer," she said. "You'll find another tabernacle, one that doesn't lead poor young girls and evil lecherous men into a life of sin."

"What life of sin?" I protested. "It's only just a couple of *hours* of sin!"

"The difference is quantitative, not qualitative," she said. "Don't you understand, Lucifer? I'm just doing what you've been telling me to do."

"I ain't never told no one to shut this place down!" I said. "Lieutenant Todd, this is all just some horrible misunderstanding. Let me and the Mademoiselle here talk things over for an hour or so and everything will be back to normal."

"I'm afraid that can't be done, Doctor Jones," said Todd. "You've got a ten-thousand-pound levy against your property for being a bawdy house, and you're going to have to put up a five-thousand-pound bond if you want to keep out of jail."

"Mademoiselle Markoff!" I pleaded. "Tell him it was all a mistake!"

"That would be a lie, Lucifer," she said, "and now that you've shown me the light I can no longer tell a lie even in a good cause, Praise God!"

"Well, at least turn over fifteen thousand pounds of my money to me so I can take care of these here legal entanglements and work things out," I said.

"I can't," she said. "I don't have a shilling."

"What are you talking about?" I bellowed. "We've took in fifty thousand pounds since I been here!"

"I gave it all to charity this afternoon, right before I went to the courthouse," she said. "The Lord wouldn't have approved of my keeping it."

"But what am I going to do?" I said.

"Well, *I've* always wanted to own a tavern and hotel," said Lieutenant Todd. "I'll be happy to purchase the place from you for, shall we say, fifteen thousand pounds."

"I paid five times that much for it!" I yelled.

"You weren't headed for the hoosegow when you bought it," he pointed out. "Think it over, Doctor Jones. Tell you what: I'll sweeten the pot by turning my back for twenty-four hours if you're of a mood to jump bail and leave the country."

Well, I haggled for half an hour or so, but he had me over a barrel, and finally I sold him the Tabernacle of Saint Luke for fifteen thousand pounds, which left me the shirt on my back (though at the time it was crumpled up on the floor) and my copy of the Good Book and not much else.

"By the way," said Todd as he took his leave of us, "if any of the girls don't feel like working in a soup kitchen, Mademoiselle Markoff, please tell them for me that my hotel can always use maids and waitresses."

He gave me a wink and walked on down the stairs.

"I hope you'll forgive me, Lucifer," said Mademoiselle Markoff when we were alone.

"That'll take a heap of doing," I said miserably.

"But if you were a less convincing preacher, none of this would have happened. I spent I don't know how many sleepless nights lusting for your body, but now that the Spirit is with me I can see that you're hardly worth all the thought I gave you."

"Thanks a lot," I grated.

"No," she said. "Thank *you* for showing me the Light and the Way."

I put on my clothes, tucked my Bible under my arm, and an hour later was marching south out of town, wishing that just this one time I hadn't been the dynamic, forceful interpreter of the Word that I unquestionably am, and making a solemn vow not to preach about anything except the racier psalms when I established my next tabernacle.

12. THE ELEPHANTS' GRAVEYARD

It didn't take me all that long to find another parish.
 I spent a couple of weeks getting clear of British East and found myself in Portuguese East Africa, which was just on the verge of changing its name to Mozambique, partially in honor of its capital city and partially because the Portuguese didn't like swamps and deserts and savages and mosquitoes and snakes and tsetse flies any more than most reasonable people and were pretty busy packing up and moving back to Portugal, where the worst thing they had to worry about was a Viking raid, of which there hadn't been none in about nine hundred years, give or take a decade.

Anyway, I had gotten about two-thirds of the way through Portuguese East, and was planning on heading down to South Africa to see if I couldn't borrow a little mission money from Emily Perrison, who was probably Emily Dobbins by now. I made it as far as the Zambezi River, which may not look like the Mississippi or the Amazon on the maps, but was just as hard to cross, especially considering that it had no bridges and about a million crocodiles, all of which had a lean and hungry look.

I was standing on the bank trying to figure out what to do next when a huge canoe loaded with black warriors pulled up just like a taxicab, and one of these painted savages gave me a big grin and gestured for me to climb in and take a ride with them.

"Thank you kindly, brothers," I said, hopping in and grabbing a seat. "I must say this is downright neighborly of you. I was afraid that I was going to have to start wrestling crocodiles for a living."

"We were happy to help a man of God," said the big fellow who had done most of the smiling. "You are a missionary, are you not?"

"Funny you should mention it," I said. "I happen to be the Reverend Doctor Jones, come to spread the Word of the Lord and otherwise brighten your dull, lackluster lives. What's for lunch?"

"We shall eat when we return to our village," said the big guy. "And after that, we would be very happy to learn about your god."

"You sure seem friendly as all get-out," I said, lighting up a cigar and offering him one, which he took. "Are you guys Zanake or Makonde?"

"Neither," he said. "We're Mangbetu."

"Mangbetu?" I said. "I thought you folks lived in the Congo."

"There was a food shortage, so some of us migrated down here."

"How'd you learn to speak English so good?"

"We've had some anthropologists come to live with us from time to time," he said. "They never stay very long, but we've picked up a smattering of French and English from them."

"I don't mean no insult," I said, "but you look pretty much like any other godless black heathens to me. Why would they single you out for serious observing and note-taking?"

"Beats me," he shrugged. "It probably has something to do with our dietary customs."

"Yeah?" I said. "What do you do that the rest of the tribes around don't do?"

"We eat people." he said.

"People?" I repeated. "Such as comes equipped with two arms and two legs and like that?"

He nodded.

"What's your philosophical and gustatory feelings about white meat?" I asked kind of nervously.

"You're our guest, Doctor Jones," he laughed. "Don't look so upset. We only eat our enemies."

Viewed that way, I could see where it could save a pile of money that would otherwise be spent on grave diggers, and would also lengthen the lives of a few innocent goats and fish, and as long as sautéed missionary wasn't one of their favorites I figured that I was just a guest and didn't want to upset no apple carts, at least not until I knew their bellies were full.

I found out that the big guy's name was Samjeba, and that he didn't mind my calling him Sam, especially when I explained that the original Samuel was Esther's cousin or manservant or chauffeur or something, and we spent a lot of time exchanging a batch of upside-down handshakes and swapping dirty stories, during which time I learned a whole lot of new Swahili words that just don't tend to crop up in the course of a normal conversation.

We arrived at the Mangbetu village a couple of hours before nightfall. The womenfolk were busy cooking up some mighty tender-looking spareribs, but in the light of our recent conversations I decided to stick to fruits and berries and easily identifiable stuff like that.

When the meal was over I got up and did a little serious preaching from the Song of Solomon, and I got an out-and-out standing ovation with a couple of British "hip hip hoorays" tossed in for good measure when I got up to Solomon 1:5, which goes: "I am black but comely, O ye daughters of Jerusalem." In fact, it took me quite some little time to explain to the more suggestible of the young bucks that Jerusalem wasn't some tribe of white women over in the next county, but was even farther away than Nairobi.

I couldn't get Sam and his people to forsake cannibalism, but I did manage to get them to agree to say grace before each meal, which was a minor triumph of sorts, especially since most of them worshiped a god who had an elephant's tusks, a woman's breasts, a lion's claws, and one hell of a cookbook.

I remained with the Mangbetus for the better part of three months, during which time I lost about twenty pounds due to an enforced diet of vegetarianism, because I never could be sure quite what kind of steaks they were cooking up at any given time. At last I couldn't stand it no more, and asked Sam if he and a couple of his better bow-and-arrow men might accompany me on a little hunting trip for klipspringer or duiker or some other kind of inoffensive and four-legged type of meat.

He agreed, and the four of us set off one sunny morning in search of a little something to fill the needs of the inner man. At least, it started off sunny; but by noontime we ran into some mighty fierce thunderstorms, so we wandered off the trail we had been following and went deeper into the jungle to get a little protection from the rain. Somehow or other we got lost, old Sam's bushcraft not quite being the equal of his talent in the kitchen, and we stayed lost throughout the rest of the day and all that night. On the morning of the next day we saw a clearing and a valley up ahead, so we headed toward it, and broke out of the forest in about twenty minutes' time.

There was some kind of smoke or fog rising, like it was some prehistoric place or something, and the first thing I noticed was all the skeletons.

"What does that look like to you, Sam?" I asked, pointing off toward the piles of bones.

"Dead elephants," he said.

"Lots of 'em," I agreed, walking down to have a closer look.

Some of them still had their tusks, and those tusks were as big as anything Herbie Miller and I ever tried to bring down back in the Lado Enclave. Others didn't have none, but I wrote it off to their being cows and pups, or whatever it is that lady elephants and their children are called.

"You know what this place is?" I said at last, turning to Sam and his two companions.

"I wish I did," admitted Sam. "Then I wouldn't feel so lost."

"This is the lost and fabled Elephants' Burial Ground, as has been writ up in song and story!" I exclaimed.

"Bad job of burying," said Sam, indicating all the skeletons that were above the ground.

"No, you got it all wrong," I said. "This is where the elephants come to die!"

Sam took another look around, and I could tell he was wondering why anyone would bother coming to such an out-of-the-way spot to die, but when I explained that it probably had something to do with their not wanting to be cooked by their enemies it made a lot more sense to him.

"Do you think you could find your way back here if you had to?" I asked.

He explained that we'd simply mark the trees on the way back to the village and we'd have no trouble, which was true, but it turned out that I had asked him the wrong question, a better one being if he knew how to find his way back to the village in the first place, but finally we got there after three or four days of hard searching.

I figured that the very first thing I had to do was stake a claim to the land that held the graveyard, and to this end I had Sam and a couple of the boys accompany me to the city of Beria on the coast, since I was sure I'd never find Sam's village again without help, let alone lead anyone to the graveyard, and while the government knew the village existed Sam kept moving it around due to various disagreements with the local constabularies concerning the finer points of his dietary laws.

Beria wasn't the most modern city on the continent, but it was a seaport, and this brought enough money in so that the government could afford to erect a couple of solid-looking brick and mud buildings from which they ran the affairs of the nation, which meant they made sure that the ships arrived and left pretty much on schedule.

One of the nice things about waterfronts is that they imply the existence of waterfront dives, and one of the nice things about waterfront dives is that if you strike up enough acquaintances and supply enough free drinks you can eventually get a line on who is the man most likely to do you some good. In this case it turned out to be Colonel Philippe Carcosa, who had risen to his imposing high rank by the simple expedient of avoiding any form of combat whatsoever while his countrymen were off dying in foreign wars or personal duels of honor.

Colonel Carcosa, so I was told, was a man who was quick to evaluate all the pros and cons of a business proposal, and who could be counted upon to act with satisfying swiftness when convinced that a handsome return on his investment could be had by so doing.

I made an appointment with the Colonel, and got an audience with him the next morning.

"Good morning," I said, walking into his luxuriously appointed office in my best Sunday preaching clothes. "I am the Right Reverend Doctor Lucifer Jones."

"Pleased to meet you, Doctor Jones," he said, rising from his polished mahogany desk and taking my hand. "May I offer you a brandy?"

"Oh, it's a little early in the day for brandy, me being a man of the cloth and all," I told him. "I think I'll settle for a double Scotch."

He grinned and had an orderly bring us each a drink.

"What can I do for you, Doctor Jones?" he asked.

"Not a hell of a lot more than I can do for you, Colonel Carcosa," I said, lighting up a cigar and offering him one, which he took.

"It's not often that I entertain the clergy in my offices," he said. "Is this in reference to a church or chapel, perhaps?"

"Close," I said. "The property I have in mind happens to be a cemetery."

"Catholic or Protestant?" he asked.

"Well, that's kind of difficult to say," I answered truthfully.

"Where is this cemetery, and what seems to he the problem?" he asked.

"I can't actually tell you where it is, and the problem is that you and me don't own it," I said. "Yet."

"And why should you and I ever wish to own a cemetery?" he asked, suddenly alert.

"Because you and me can't see no reason whatsoever why we shouldn't be millionaires," I told him.

"That is true," he said, nodding thoughtfully. "No matter how earnestly I search my heart, I simply cannot come up with an acceptable reason. Now, my friend, perhaps you might be willing to explain why the possession of this particular cemetery will substantially alter our financial situation."

"Certainly," I said, taking another sip of my drink. "Colonel Carcosa, I have discovered the lost burial ground of the elephants!"

"I didn't even know it was missing," he said.

"This is the place where all the elephants go to die," I said. "It's just chock full of skeletons, most of them loaded down with ivory, and it just stands to reason that as long as elephants keep feeling the need to die they'll keep going to the burial ground and adding to the treasure that awaits us there."

Colonel Carcosa signaled for his aide. "No more liquor for Doctor Jones," he said. "He doesn't seem to be able to handle it."

"But it's true!" I said. "I saw it with my own eyes!"

"This is the silliest story I have ever heard in a long lifetime of hearing silly stories," he said. "I'm afraid I must ask you to leave."

"Wait!" I cried. "If I take you there and let you see it yourself, are we partners?"

"What are you talking about?" he said.

"We got to buy that graveyard before anyone else stakes a claim!" I said. "I ain't got no money, but I know where it is; you don't know where it is, but you can put up the money. If I can convince you it really exists, do we have a deal?"

"How far is it from here?" he asked suspiciously.

"About six days' march," I said.

He pulled a map out of his desk. "Mark its location," he said.

"I can't," I said.

"Then how are we to find this mythical graveyard?" he demanded.

"I got three Mangbetus waiting for me outside of town," I said. "They were with me when I discovered it. They can show us the way."

"Mangbetus?" he said, his eyebrows raised.

"Right," I said. "And a God-fearing race they are, except in matters of diet."

"You know, I could arrest you for coming to me with a harebrained scheme like this," he said.

"True, Brother Carcosa," I said. "But then I'd just have to go out and find another partner once you set me free, and I truly don't see how that could possibly benefit either of us."

"All right," he said. "Come back here tomorrow morning and I will be ready to leave with you. But if this graveyard does not exist, it is going to go very hard with you, Doctor Jones. Very hard indeed."

"Brother Carcosa," I said, rising and shaking his hand, "you got yourself a deal."

I picked him up the next morning, and we were joined by Sam and the boys when we got a couple of miles west of the city limits. I knew he wasn't all that thrilled with the Mangbetu tribe, but I warned him to keep it under his hat, because the very last thing anyone in his right mind would want was to be viewed as an enemy by the Mangbetus, especially if they had a little mustard and onions handy. He took it under advisement, and the following six days were kind of routine.

Colonel Carcosa had a big map folded up in his backpack, and every couple of hours he'd pull it out and make certain notations on it. When we finally got to Sam's village he made us spend an extra day there while he checked out various landmarks to make sure he had the place spotted on the map. Then we spent a couple more days hunting up the graveyard, but we finally found it despite Sam's deficiencies at bushcraft.

"By God, Doctor Jones!" exclaimed Colonel Carcosa. "I must confess that until this minute I really didn't believe you!"

"Then why did you come along?" I asked as we moseyed down into the valley.

"If nothing else, I could always have turned the Mangbetus in for the reward," he said. Sam kind of tensed at that, and started looking at the Colonel the way a chef looks at a choice piece of tenderloin, but the Colonel simply smiled back and said, "Of course, that won't be necessary now, especially in view of the fact that we're going to need a nonstop stream of highly-paid porters."

That soothed Sam down a bit, and after a while he looked like he might settle for maybe only cutting off two or three of the Colonel's toes to flavor up a stew or something.

We walked down to the skeletons, and started counting, and came up with seven elephants.

"But that's just what's on the surface," said the Colonel. "There's no telling how many have sunk under the soft moist ground. Possibly thousands."

"Not only that," I pointed out, "but we might not even be safe standing right here. I mean, for all we know there's a couple of dozen elephants making their way here right now just to die on this very spot."

He thought about that for a moment and then walked a few feet away. I nodded my approval and told him he looked much safer in his new location.

"Well, Doctor Jones," he said after a few minutes, "I've seen enough. Let's get back to Beria and stake a claim to this place before anybody else stumbles onto it."

That made a lot of sense to me, especially since there were a few million army ants discussing combat strategy and logistics a couple of hundred yards away. So we went back to the Mangbetu village very slowly, with the Colonel marking things down on his map every half mile or so. We rested up for a day and then, accompanied only by Sam, who came along mainly to guide me back after we'd claimed the place, we returned to Beria.

I took a room in a local hostelry, Sam hung around a nearby restaurant getting hints on different ways to soften meat, and Colonel Carcosa went to the proper authorities to purchase the tract of land that contained the burial ground. He was in a real good mood when we met for dinner.

"Did you get it?" I asked as soon as he had pulled up a chair.

"Of course," he said.

"No problems?" I said. "Nobody suspects nothing?"

"Doctor Jones, you're not dealing with an amateur," he replied smugly. "The graveyard was in the middle of a privately owned two-hundred-thousand-acre tract of land. I purchased the whole thing at five British shillings an acre."

"The whole thing?" I said. "But why?"

"Because if it were known that I had bought one hundred acres or so in the interior of Portuguese East Africa, it would arouse curiosity. But two hundred thousand acres? It might seem peculiar, but no one is going to race out to search every square centimeter of the land to find out what I want with it."

I opined as to how it made a bit of sense at that, and we spent the rest of the evening toasting each other's good health and success in the world of high finance.

The next morning Sam and I set out for the graveyard, armed with saws and such other equipment as we might need to separate the various tusks from their skeletons. We stopped off at the Mangbetu village long enough to recruit a little help and for Sam to refresh Missus Sam, and then we headed off for the burial ground. Four of the skeletons had tusks, and we removed them and toted them all the way back to Mozambique.

"Excellent," said Colonel Carcosa, when the tusks averaged out at one hundred thirty pounds apiece. "I've ordered some earth-moving equipment which should be here in about four months, at which time we can begin digging up all the skeletons that have sunk into the muck and mire."

It made sense to me, and I prepared to spend the next four months loafing and sleeping and enjoying the company of the local ladies, but Colonel Carcosa started getting itchy a few days later and sent me and Sam off to pick up the tusks from any new corpses.

I got back to Beria two weeks later with the news that there weren't any new corpses.

"That's very odd," said the Colonel. "After all, it's been almost a month since I was there. You would think some elephants would have died since then."

"Maybe this ain't the season for it," I suggested.

"And maybe you are being less than honest with me," he said accusingly.

"Brother Carcosa," I said. "I been telling you nothing but God's own truth. If you don't believe me, come on right now and we'll march out there together."

He stared long and hard at me, as if he was making up his mind. "I'll trust you for the moment," he announced at last, "but if I should ever find out that you were stealing ivory from our property, Doctor Jones, I have the power to make the rest of your life very unpleasant."

Getting threatened by your partner can be pretty thirsty work, so after he finished talking I moseyed on over to the local pub, where I ordered a bottle of beer, and started carrying it to a table in the corner.

"Well, if it ain't the Reverend Lucifer Jones!" hollered a familiar voice.

I turned and saw Capturing Clyde Calhoun sitting at the bar.

"I sure didn't expect to see you here, Clyde," I said, walking over and joining him. "I figured your circus would be taking you to Bucharest and Rotterdam and all them other glittering exotic capitals of Europe."

"I'll be joining the circus in a couple of days," said Calhoun, pouring himself a glass of rye whiskey and offering one to me. "I'm just here to ship some survivors back to various zoos in the States."

"Well, it sure is good to see a friendly face," I said. "How's Lord Bloomstoke getting along?"

"Just fine," replied Calhoun. "Of course, I've had to land on him a couple of times about organizing the monkeys, but other than that he's doing a right creditable job. And how about yourself, Reverend? You ever get that tabernacle?"

I told him the sad story of the Tabernacle of Saint Luke, and then he told me the sad story of how he figured out that he had a career waiting for him in the Dark Continent on the day he accidentally shot the mayor's horse back in Billings, Montana, and then I told him the sad story of losing the affections of Miss Emily Perrison to Major Theodore Dobbins, late of His Majesty's armed forces, and then he told me the sad story of his first five wives.

"We've sure had our share of bad luck, ain't we, Clyde?" I said, starting to feel downright weepy.

"We sure have," he agreed.

"I don't mean to butt in, gents," said the bartender. "But I got a hard-luck story to match anything you've got. I used to be a hunter like Mister Calhoun here."

"What happened?" I asked, ordering another beer and pouring two shots of rye into it, just to bring out the subtle nuances of its flavor.

"I got flim-flammed so bad I had to take this here bartending job to climb out from under a mountain of debts that I had taken on in good faith," said the bartender. "Seems this fellow hired me to go to some valley out in the middle of nowhere, right next to some cannibal sanctuary about five or six days' march from here, and offered me a thousand pounds for every elephant I could lure there and shoot. Then, after I'd spent a couple of weeks fighting off mosquitoes and hornets and tsetse flies and black mambas and the like and had actually shot a batch of elephants, I came back to town here and wrote notes against the money I was owed, but the son of a bitch took off and I never saw him or heard from him again."

"How much did he owe you?" I asked with a sinking feeling in the pit of my stomach.

"Seven thousand pounds!" said the bartender. "And of course we were so far out in the middle of the bush he knew there was no way for me and my one gun bearer to bring any of that ivory back to civilization."

"Did he say why he wanted you to shoot the elephants?" asked Calhoun.

"I gather he'd just bought a couple hundred thousand acres at a penny an acre or some such ridiculous price, and he seemed to think that leaving a bunch of dead elephants at this particular spot would make his real estate appreciate. I told him and told him that ivory ain't like flowers and that you can't just leave it on the ground and hope it'll take root and multiply, but he just kind of chuckled and said he was a patient man and that sooner or later someone would be impressed by the fact that I'd killed all them elephants. I dunno; I guess he thought shooting elephants in that stupid little valley would make it a national historic shrine or something."

"This feller's name didn't happen to have a Germanic sound to it, did it?" I asked, feeling kind of weak about the knees.

"Sure as hell did," said the bartender.

"What was it?" I asked.

"Von Horst," he replied.

"Damn!" I moaned. "I *knew* it!"

"Yep. Erich Von Horst it was," continued the bartender. "I'll remember that name to my dying day."

"You got lots of company," I said.

I explained to Capturing Clyde that I suddenly remembered that I had urgent business elsewhere, and made a beeline toward Sam's favorite restaurant, where I told him that we should give serious thought to leaving the country at the earliest possible opportunity, like right that moment.

He told me that we'd be better off stopping by his village one last time so he could pick up some warriors to defend us against the denizens of the jungle and take along enough women to keep us all happy. I told him that I appreciated the thought, but right now I was a little more concerned with one particular denizen of the Portuguese East African government. He told me that he'd like to accommodate me, but it wouldn't be fair to the Mangbetu tribe as a whole for him to leave the country without sharing his newfound cooking knowledge with them.

Well, I could see I wasn't going to talk him out of it, and it made more sense to start walking toward the village right away than to spend all night standing in the street arguing, so I fell into step and we reached the village some six days later.

Sam conducted a three-hour graduate cooking seminar, gathered the people he thought we'd be most in need of, and headed off toward Tanganyika. We must have been within two miles of the border when a group of about twenty Portuguese soldiers, all armed to the teeth, intercepted us.

Sam was willing to fight to the death, but I explained to him that I had a feeling that the soldiers weren't really after the Mangbetu. The soldier nearest to us nodded, so I wished Sam and his people *bon appetit* as they retreated into the bush. My hands were chained behind me and I was marched all the way back to Beria, where I spent nine days in jail and was then brought to the office of an elderly gentleman named Alfredo Montenegro, who happened to hold the position of Chief Justice.

"Ah, Doctor Jones," he said. "I have been wondering exactly what you looked like. Now at long last I have the pleasure of making your acquaintance."

"It's a pleasure you could have had eight and a half days sooner as far as I'm concerned," I told him.

"You led us a merry little chase," he noted pleasantly. "There were times when I despaired of ever capturing you."

"Come to think of it, how *did* you know we'd be where we were?" I asked.

"Most armies travel on their stomachs, Doctor Jones," he said. "Let us say that a cannibalistic army is just a tad easier to trace than certain others might be."

"Poor heathen must of backslid," I said. "Sam promised me they were only going to practice it as a ritual."

"Eating can be as ritualistic as most things," noted Montenegro. "But here you are safe and sound in Beria, so why bother yourself with how you came to be here?"

"True enough," I said. "But perhaps you might tell me why a man of the cloth who never meant no harm to nobody should have been held in durance vile for lo these many days?"

"My dear Doctor Jones," he said, "we may be an old colonial power, but we are not yet senile. When we discovered that a block of two hundred thousand acres had changed hands we started piercing through the corporate veil and came up with your friend Colonel Carcosa. We discovered, in tracing back over his actions, that he had spent a considerable amount of time in your company, and began reconstructing what you two had been up to. It all fell into place after we had a little chat with a fellow countryman of yours, a circus owner who thought he was helping your cause and incriminating a gentleman with a Germanic name who is of no importance to this case."

"Well, if you know all about it," I replied, "then you know that we were flim-flammed ourselves, and that there ain't no such thing as an elephants' graveyard. So that ought to let us off the hook, right?"

"*Wrong!*" he thundered. "Doctor Jones, conspiracy with intent to defraud is every bit as much a criminal offense as fraud itself, and is punishable under very stringent laws, as your friend the former officer is currently finding out."

"You mean you're going to lock me up for a deal that cost me and my partner a million shillings?" I demanded.

"We would prefer not to," he said. "After all, you are an American citizen, and we don't wish to cause your government any distress or embarrassment."

"Well, then, just let me go and we'll let bygones be bygones and I'll forget the whole thing ever happened," I said magnanimously.

"It's not as easy as all that," said Montenegro. "Your presence is no longer desired in Portuguese East Africa."

"Never fear," I said. "I'll just take my copy of the Good Book and such members of my Mangbetu flock as remain loyal to me in my hour of need and clear out lock, stock, and barrel."

"I'm afraid that's out of the question," he said, shaking his head slowly.

"What's the problem?" I said. "There's lots of other countries around that'd be proud to have a missionary preaching the Word to the poor uneducated heathen."

"Doctor Jones," he said slowly, "while you were our . . . ah . . . guest, we made certain inquiries of our neighboring nations concerning their reaction should we decide to expel you."

"And?" I said.

"You are wanted in South Africa, Bechuanaland, and the Transvaal for selling fraudulent treasure maps. There is a warrant out for your arrest in Egypt for slave trading and certain illegal practices involving a mummy. You are wanted in Morocco and Algeria for grand larceny involving the theft of a diamond known as the Lion's Tooth."

"But I didn't steal it!" I protested. "Hell, I didn't even know I *had* it!"

"Please don't interrupt. You are wanted in the Lado Enclave and Uganda for ivory poaching. You are wanted for removing certain national treasures in the form of precious stones from Nyasaland. The nation of Southwest Africa has issued a warrant for your arrest for killing whales without a license."

"A series of misunderstandings, nothing more," I said.

"Let me continue," he said. "You are wanted in Kenya for operating a bawdy house. The Congo has issued a warrant for your arrest for possible complicity in the disappearance of a gentleman named Burley Rourke. The Sudan wishes to speak to you about slave trading and impersonating a British officer and war hero, and Tanganyika is after you for consorting with known criminals." He paused and stared at me. "Frankly, Doctor Jones, I wonder where you find the energy to get through the day."

"How about Rhodesia?" I said. "I ain't never been there."

"Both Rhodesias have extradition treaties with all of the nations I have mentioned."

"Then what are you going to do with me?" I asked.

"It is my opinion that the entire continent of Africa will be better off without your particular brand of salvation," he said slowly. "Therefore, if you will agree to accept passage out of here tomorrow morning, I'll see to it that you are placed aboard a ship before any other African government can officially request that we detain you."

"I don't see as to how I've got much of a choice," I said. "As long as I've got to go, Brother Montenegro, how about getting me on a boat today so's I don't have to spend another night in jail?"

"Nothing would make me happier than getting you out of Beria today," he said, "but the only passenger ship currently in port is *The*

Dying Quail, and for reasons I can only guess at, they refuse to allow you aboard."

So I spent my last night in Africa pretty much the same way I had spent some of my first ones.

My spirits were at an all-time low when they took me to the ship the next afternoon. I'd made three or four quick fortunes, only to be gulled out of them by sinful, godless men, and I had even had my beloved tabernacle ripped from my hands by a cruel and unfeeling Fate.

"*Eli, Eli, lama sabachthani?*" I muttered as I started climbing up the gangplank without a penny to my name and carrying no luggage except my well-worn copy of the Good Book.

I paused halfway between shore and ship and turned to take a last look at the Dark Continent. I'd met a lot of interesting folk there, and done most of them more good than they had done me. If it hadn't been for me and me alone, Herbie Miller and the Rodent would still be looking for jobs, and the Dutchman, Ali ben Ishak, Major Theodore Dobbins, Ishmael Bledsoe, and Luthor Christian would all still be hunting for spouses. Rosepetal Schultz would still be selling her dubious services in the back alleys of Cairo, Friday would be wearing a loincloth and living out in the bush, Lord Bloomstoke would still be hiding from his creditors, Capturing Clyde Calhoun would have lowered the world's gorilla population by half, and Mademoiselle Markoff wouldn't have seen the Glory and the Light.

All in all, I decided, it wasn't a bad four years' work at that. I'd left my mark on a whole bunch of previously worthless lives, and I was still young and vigorous and with my whole life ahead of me.

"You can keep this damned hellhole, Von Horst!" I hollered into the wind. "I'm going off to strange new lands where a God-fearing Christian can still make an honest living!"

I climbed up the rest of the gangplank and was about to hunt up my cabin when my eyes fell on one of the passengers, a vision of loveliness who looked like a redheaded version of Rosepetal Schultz, and the human spirit, glorious and unquenchable thing that it is, began to soar within me once again, especially after I saw the size of the diamonds on her necklace. I stopped to introduce myself and offer her any form of spiritual comfort or uplifting that might appeal to her. She giggled and agreed to discuss the matter more fully over dinner, and by the time the voyage was over we had become fast friends. In fact, truth to tell, it was occasionally a race between us to see just which of us was the faster.

We landed in the far exotic Orient, where sinful and mysterious cities like Hong Kong and Macao and Singapore and Shanghai, all filled with godless men and women and dens of vice and rebel armies and the like, were just waiting for a handsome young buck like myself to come and bring the Word to them, a task to which I dedicated the next few years of my life with considerable success.

But that, of course, is another story.

℘ The End (Volume One) ☙

Available September 28, 2011

www.PhoenixPick.com

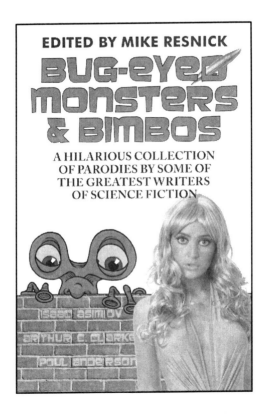

Isaac Asimov, Arthur C. Clarke, Poul Anderson
& Many More

Guaranteed to make you laugh out loud, again & again.